KV-433-441

Contents

Overview

Public services face huge challenges, if they are to deliver the improvements that users expect. During its first term, the Government put in place a range of reforms intended to stimulate improvement in services across central and local government, and in the NHS. More reform is promised for the second term. This makes change management one of the key skills needed by leaders of public services.

At the Commission, we have learned a great deal about both the opportunities and the challenges of managing change effectively, through our work with local public service bodies. This paper seeks to distil that learning, as well as drawing on the insights of successful leaders of change, to help public service managers to rise to the challenge of delivering continuous improvement for service users.

It is only by focusing on users' experience that public services can deliver improvements that are relevant and add public value. This means that successful change programmes must begin and end with an understanding of what matters to users.

Change initiatives must be 'bespoke tailored' by local organisations to tackle the problems facing their communities, if change is to be 'owned' locally by the public and by their own staff. This does not mean accepting variations in performance that compromise service outcomes. Communities everywhere expect the same high standards of health, education, and policing, provided by the best performers. However, it does mean that change cannot be driven from the centre alone. The Government must give local service providers the flexibility to respond to local demands. In return, public service bodies must deliver excellent services that match the standards of the best.

Change Here!

Managing Change to Improve Local Services

INTRODUCING

Change Here!

Managing Change to Improve Local Services

Managing change is one of the greatest challenges facing public services. Public service leaders have no option but to improve users' experience of services if public and political expectations are to be met. So, at all levels of the public sector, people are asking questions about how to manage and lead change to achieve sustained performance gains.

The purpose of *Change Here!*

Through its audit, research and inspection activities, both alone and in partnership with others, the Audit Commission has accumulated considerable experience of how local bodies can manage change successfully and overcome barriers to improving services. This knowledge has been drawn together in *Change Here!*, a guide for top managers in local government and the NHS, who are responsible for delivering services to their communities. An interactive web-based tool is also available at www.audit-commission.gov.uk/changehere. This provides a quick and engaging route into the guide's key ideas, and helps users to find and explore topics and case studies of particular interest.

The material in *Change Here!* is based on practical experience of change management in both the public and private sectors. It draws very selectively from academic literature and builds on a series of interactive workshops where managers, change experts and Audit Commission staff shared and explored their experiences of making change happen in public services. It is illustrated with local examples, which highlight some of the key lessons and show how they have been applied in practice in a variety of situations. It is intended as a reasonably light and interesting read for chief executives and their executive teams as they steer

their own local organisations through change. It may lead local teams to reflect upon how they themselves are managing change, and perhaps to take stock of their current approaches and identify some things they could do differently. The *Change Here!* web-based tool is particularly good for this purpose. Insofar as it describes the change process and highlights the key issues for local leaders to consider, *Change Here!* is likely to be of interest to politicians, non-executives and policymakers, who also need a sound understanding of change processes. Finally, *Change Here!* will be relevant to organisation, strategy, human resource and knowledge and information specialists, and others in corporate roles who are concerned with organisational change.

All around us, public service leaders are struggling with conflicting demands and unrealistic expectations from politicians, the public and their own staff. While there is no magic formula for managing change, there is a body of useful experience about what works that can help top managers to improve services today and build long-term capacity for the future. Although the key lessons from *Change Here!* are not in themselves revolutionary, evidence suggests that public service leaders would welcome more help to understand their full implications and translate them into practice (see exhibit below).

ATTITUDES TO CHANGE AMONG LOCAL STAFF

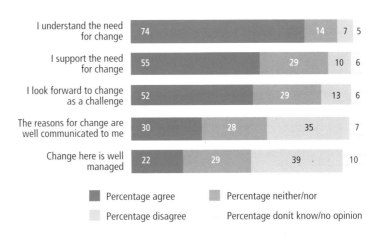

Source: MORI (Sharing A Vision, 2000) Question: To what extent do you agree or disagree with the following statements?

KEY MESSAGES

Change Here! suggests seven lessons for leadership teams as they steer their organisations through major change programmes.

- Change leadership is about developing and promoting a shared vision, mobilising staff and stakeholder support, and navigating and supporting the organisation through the change journey.

- Successful leaders spend huge amounts of time communicating and building support for change.

- Leaders need persistence, resilience and consistency of purpose to stick to the key priorities through the typical ups and downs of change.

- To improve the things that matter, change programmes must be rooted in users' experiences and priorities.

- Weak project management is often to blame when change programmes fail.

- Leaders can use external input as a key lever and support for change.

- Change programmes should include building the capacity for continuous improvement as an explicit goal.

Change Here! develops these themes and includes tools and approaches to help leadership teams to translate them into action.

Future products

The Commission is very interested in learning more about the experiences of public service leaders who are managing change. By further developing its understanding of change management issues, the Commission hopes to make a continuing contribution to the thinking in this field, and also to refine and develop its own approaches to supporting public service improvement. It is currently developing a future programme of publications and events on the theme of change management and would like to hear from interested organisations about where the Commission's contribution might add most value. If you have any feedback on this paper or would like to share your own organisation's experience of managing change, please contact the Commission's Performance Development Directorate by letter, telephone or email to changehere@audit-commission.gov.uk by 30 September 2001.

To order *Change Here!*

To order copies of *Change Here!*, please telephone **0800 502030**. Or complete the order form below and send to **Audit Commission Publications, PO Box 99, Wetherby LS23 7JA, fax 0870 1214217**.

TITLE	ISBN	STOCK CODE	QUANTITY	PRICE	TOTAL PRICE
Change Here!	1862402752	GMP1804		£25	

*UK: £2 for one report, £3.25 for two or more reports.
Overseas: price on application, telephone 44 1937 840779.

*CARRIAGE	
GRAND TOTAL	

☐ Please invoice me at the address below (purchase order number required)

☐ I enclose a cheque made payable to Two Ten Communications

☐ I authorise you to debit my credit card VISA/Mastercard (delete as applicable)

Card number /___/___/___/___/___/___/___/___/___/___/___/___/___/___/___/___/

Cardholder's name   **Cardholder's signature**

Mr/Mrs/Ms/Other   **Initials**   **Surname**

Job Title   **Organisation**

Address

                                            Postcode

Telephone   **Fax**   **Email address**

Purchase order number   **Date of order**

☐ Please tick here if you do not wish to be added to the Audit Commission's mailing list.

REFERENCE: CH1234567

Achieving the transformational change that leads to excellence demands a relentless focus on a small number of key priorities, as well as commitment by public service bodies to maintain this focus through the inevitable highs and lows of the change process. The Government can support this focus by setting out clearly its priorities for improvement, and giving local public service bodies the space and freedoms to deliver them.

Above all, leaders of local public services play a crucial role in maintaining a commitment to major change initiatives, by mobilising and sustaining support for change among staff and local stakeholders. By setting out a clear vision, and investing in effective ways to communicate this to staff, leaders can keep their organisations on track through the change journey.

Delivering positive change and continuous service improvement is the biggest challenge facing public services. Managers and non-executives also face a major task in balancing national priorities alongside the concerns of local communities.

At the Commission, we will continue to support local services in their drive to achieve excellence. But it is public service leaders, above all else, who can make this step-change happen. By providing a clear sense of purpose, and inspiring the commitment of staff, public services can be transformed. We look forward to working with you to achieve this shared ambition.

Sir Andrew Foster
Controller

1. Introduction

Context

The purpose of this paper

Four types of change

Key points

Context

1.   As we move into the 21st century, the public sector is faced with the
challenge to improve the service it delivers to its customers. Over the
past decade or so, most of us have experienced sizeable leaps in the
quality, choice and accessibility of services we take for granted as part
of our daily lives. But a gap has opened up between what commercial
services can deliver and what we can expect from public services. For
example, two-thirds of the people in this country now own mobile
telephones and the cost of calls has fallen by nearly one-quarter over
the past two years. We can buy cheap fresh food from around the world
at any time of the day or night at a local supermarket or, if we prefer,
over the phone or pc, to minimise interruption to the 40 or so television
channels transmitted into our homes. Meanwhile, it is still difficult to
find a public library open before or after work or at any time on
Sundays, and GP surgery hours are similarly limited. This may be
acceptable to the generation that remembers the hardship of life
without decent public services. But for increasing numbers of us today,
despite the effort and commitment of public service workers, the
widening gulf between what we can buy as customers and what we get
as public service users has created a credibility gap. As a result, many
have become alienated from the political process and disaffected with
public services in general.

2.   This is not to dismiss the progress that public services have made,
nor the talent and commitment of staff, managers and leaders. Charged
with meeting multiple objectives, public services face greater challenges
and have more restricted resources than is fairly reflected by a straight
comparison with industry. Moreover, the public sector must serve all
sections of society, not just those with money in their pockets. During
the past 30 years, attitudes to public services have evolved from a
paternalistic assumption that the state will provide, through stringent
public spending restraint and wholesale privatisation, to the current
philosophy that accepts an underlying societal responsibility for good
public services but increasingly expects empowered individuals to take
responsibility for themselves. This reality is full of contradictions:
between local autonomy and central control, between consumer
expectations and the capacity of services that have been starved of

investment, between what people say they want and what they are prepared to pay for.

3. As services fall short of public and political expectation, the modernisation agenda calls for significant improvement in performance throughout the public sector [EXHIBIT 1, overleaf]. Best value in local government is being matched by a plethora of initiatives within the NHS Plan.[1] But experienced managers know that delivering tangible change on the ground goes well beyond policymaking. Nor is it primarily about structural reorganisation, which can be simultaneously energy-sapping and irrelevant to the primary task of improving services. Change is not a simple, linear process, and numerous examples illustrate how difficult it is to achieve sustained improvement in public services [CASE STUDY 1, overleaf]. Improving the experience of users, patients and their families requires not only changes to systems and procedures in what are often huge, complex and interdependent organisations, but also, crucially, changes to the attitudes and behaviour of individual members of staff. Change is painful and destructive as well as positive and creative. It challenges vested interests: personal, professional and institutional. Change is unavoidable; potentially both exciting and rewarding, but at the same time a messy and difficult enterprise, frequently confounding the intentions of managers, politicians and policymakers.

4. All around us, public service leaders are struggling with conflicting demands and unrealistic expectations from politicians, the public and within their own organisations. There is no magic formula for change management, but there is a body of useful experience about what works that can help top management to improve services today and build long-term capacity for the future.

Introduction

9

Context

NHS Plan: A Plan for Investment, A Plan for Reform, Department of Health, 2000.

EXHIBIT 1   EXPECTATIONS FOR PUBLIC SERVICES

The modernisation agenda calls for significant improvement in performance throughout the public sector.

"At every level there will be radical change"
Prime Minister, NHS Plan

"[Best value] will make a vital difference to the quality and effectiveness of local services"
Local Government Minister

"Over the next few years patients will see major improvements in their local health services"
Secretary of State for Health, NHS Plan

CASE STUDY 1   INTRODUCING ELECTRONIC PATIENT RECORDS

Background: Inadequate patient records are a major source of risk and avoidable cost in hospitals. Patient care is jeopardised and professional time wasted by inaccurate, illegible or lost paper records because the correct information is not available at the time and point of decision making.

Impact: Introducing electronic patient records (EPR) would help to reduce risk and cost, supporting other systems such as automated test results and electronic prescribing. The technology to deliver EPR in hospitals has been around for more than ten years, but only a handful of hospitals have implemented these systems successfully. Meanwhile, research has shown that 11 per cent of patients experience an 'adverse event' while in hospital, one-third of which lead to greater disability or death. Each adverse event leads to an average of eight extra days in hospital, costing the NHS an additional £1.1 billion a year in total.

Critical factors

Introducing EPR is a particularly complex challenge requiring a number of significant barriers to be overcome. The reasons why successful implementation has not been more widespread include:

- inability to sustain commitment to EPR in the face of other more urgent priorities;

- failure to place the systems development within a local vision for improving services to patients;

- no concerted communication effort to convince politicians and the public of the value of spending money on support systems rather than front-line care initiatives;

- insufficient emphasis on changing the behaviour of large numbers of staff across the full range of clinical specialities; and

- failure to protect additional resources for the new systems.

The purpose of this paper

5. At all levels of the public sector, people are asking questions about how to manage and lead change successfully. The sheer size and range of the academic and management literature on change can be daunting, particularly as few models have been rigorously evaluated. The National Co-ordinating Centre for NHS Service Delivery and Organisation R&D (NCCSDO) aims to help practitioners to find their way through the literature with its recent series of publications.[1] This paper is intended as a guide to change for top managers of local government and NHS bodies who are responsible for delivering services to their communities.

6. Clearly, chief executives in the NHS and local government work within different organisational, legislative and political contexts, and face different challenges in their approach to change. For local government, the local political dimension is crucial. For leaders in the

---

I   *Organisational Change: A review for managers, professionals and researchers*, Iles and Sutherland, 2001. There is also a companion booklet, *Different and Better?: Learning from change in the health service*, and reference card, *Making Informed Decisions on Change: Key points for managers and professionals*.

NHS, many of the most difficult issues lie in the relationships between professional groups and an overload of priorities from the centre. Increasingly, having an impact on the most intractable public service issues means managing change across organisational boundaries and in partnership with others. Nevertheless, there is a core set of challenges in delivering successful change, whether it is in social services, education, the NHS, police, fire or indeed across all large and complex organisations, both public and private. It is these core challenges that this paper addresses.

7. The material is based on the Audit Commission's accumulated understanding, through its experience of audit, research and inspection, both alone and in partnership with others, of how local bodies can manage change successfully and overcome barriers to improving services. It is derived from practical experience of change management in both public and private sectors. It also draws very selectively from the academic literature and builds on a series of interactive workshops where managers, change experts and Audit Commission staff shared and explored their experiences of making change happen in public services. It is illustrated with examples, chosen to highlight some of the key lessons and show how they have been applied in practice. It is intended as a reasonably quick and interesting read for chief executives and their executive teams as they steer their own local organisations through the change process. It may lead local teams to reflect upon how they themselves are managing change, and perhaps to take stock of their approach and identifying some things to do differently. The package includes this paper and an interactive web-based tool which presents the key concepts in an accessible form and includes a library of case studies (available at www.audit-commission.gov.uk/changehere).

8. Insofar as they describe the change process and highlight the key issues for local leaders to consider, the paper and website are likely also to be of interest to politicians, non-executives and policymakers, who themselves need a sound understanding of change processes. Finally, it will be relevant to organisation, strategy, human resource and knowledge and information specialists and others in corporate roles who are concerned with organisational change. The Commission is very interested to learn more about the experiences of public service leaders who have been managing change. If you have any feedback on this paper or would like to share your own organisation's experience of the change process, please contact the Commission's Performance Development Directorate by letter, telephone or email to changehere@audit-commission.gov.uk

9. This introductory section concludes with a definition of four broad types of change and highlights the transformational model as most challenging and relevant for today's public services. The following chapter explores the role of leadership in delivering performance improvement. The remaining material is organised into six sections on key aspects of change management, each covering ideas that people have found useful in achieving change and overcoming barriers to service improvement.

Four types of change

10. Part of the debate surrounding change management focuses on the question, "what kind of change is this?" People commonly distinguish step-change – often seen as linear and top-down – from continuous improvement – generally depicted as an ongoing cycle, with the momentum more likely to come from the grass roots of the organisation. A simple, helpful way of categorising change is to think about two dimensions: how *radical*: step-change or incremental; and how *centrally controlled*: directive or organic. Combining the two dimensions gives four broad types of change, as described by Ruddle and Feeny,[1] whose relevance depends on the current performance of the organisation and the predictability or otherwise of its environment [EXHIBIT 2, overleaf]. Each type of change has its place. One organisation may need to go through different types of change at different times as its performance improves or deteriorates and external conditions change. The important thing is that the **process** fits the **purpose**.

---

1   *Transforming the Organisation: New approaches to management, measurement and leadership*, Ruddle and Feeny, 1997.

EXHIBIT 2   FOUR TYPES OF CHANGE

Transformation is the most relevant type of change for many public services today.

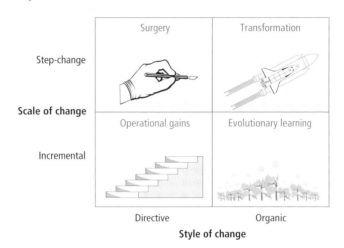

Style of change

Incremental-directive: operational gains

- Successful organisations in stable environments can go for operational gains where change is programmed in detail with a controlled and monitored approach. Stability is a prerequisite for this kind of change because it is centrally driven and does not rely on bottom-up learning and live feedback about how things work in practice, or how customer needs or external conditions are evolving. Given the right conditions, it is less risky and lower cost than other approaches. It can be useful for driving down costs and raising productivity. However, it does not tend to work forever: there comes a time when the external world moves on and an organisation that relies exclusively on programmed operational gains will find itself out of step with customers or, in the commercial world, eclipsed by competitors.

Step-directive: surgery

- Where a radical shift is needed, objectives are clear and can be tightly monitored and the environment is predictable with defined goals for the organisation, a highly planned and prescriptive approach can be successful. This might be described as 'marching out of a crisis' or 'strategic surgery'. It works best in relatively simple organisations or in clearly identifiable business units within a larger and more complex whole. The National Literacy Strategy is an example of this approach. Turning around a failing direct labour organisation would be another. It requires concentrated energy and determination on the part of the leadership team to overcome resistance, and often involves drastic steps, including the loss of many jobs. The organisation that emerges at the end of such a process may be very different from the one that went in, but the hearts and minds of the individuals within it may not have moved on to the same extent.

Step-organic: transformation

- The most challenging conditions are a need for much better performance in an environment of continuing uncertainty. Here transformational change is called for, where visionary leadership and a broad cross-section of management must own the process and work together to identify and follow the path for the journey. Change is initiated and led from the top, but detailed changes in working practices emerge through a process that engages and involves many people throughout the organisation. Transformation may be kicked off on a broad front, touching on all parts of the organisation at the same time. This is the riskiest approach, and few organisations can cope successfully with the upheaval it creates. An alternative and less risky route to transformation is to select one or more targeted areas to work on first. The initial project/s should ideally involve significant cross-functional change and pave the way towards the overall vision, such as becoming a more customer-focused organisation. The changes needed to deliver these major projects can then unlock the potential for further dynamic shifts through, for example, introducing new ways of working; developing new capabilities; establishing more flexible personnel policies; developing people; delegating greater responsibility to operational staff; upgrading the technology platform; and providing essential learning about managing the process of change. Several local authorities are currently engaged in this type of change [CASE STUDY 2]

Incremental-organic: evolutionary learning

- Where the organisation is clear about its strategic direction and is performing well, but operates in an uncertain environment with a lack of well-understood good practice to draw on, evolutionary learning at all levels of the organisation enables progressive experimentation, focusing on the user. This approach could work for police basic command units as local crime patterns change, for example, or for primary care trusts as they become established. It is often appropriate for organisations that have come through transformation: having achieved high performance levels, they then need to keep innovating to remain at the leading edge. Such evolutionary learning can succeed until a discontinuity in the external environment, perhaps several years down the line, which precipitates a fundamental strategy review that could in turn lead to a further phase of transformation.

CASE STUDY 2   LEADING AN ORGANISATION OUT OF CRISIS

Background: Liverpool City Council is in the process of transforming itself from one of the worst performing local authorities in the country into a well-run organisation that is capable of delivering quality services to the people of Liverpool.

Approach: An effective partnership between political and managerial leaders is helping the city council reverse 30 years of organisational decline. The leader and new chief executive began their campaign by setting out a vision of Liverpool as a Premier European City. Raising aspirations and building confidence helped to sustain the city council while it transformed a failing organisation. An entirely new top executive team was recruited to overturn the deeply rooted culture of departmentalism, antagonism, mistrust and outright hostility between different departments and between senior officers and members. Executive directors now have individual responsibility for priority areas that cut across traditional departmental boundaries. By spending concentrated time together off-site, leading members and senior officers have built trust and developed and published a set of values. The chief executive and five executive directors operate on the principle that "if you talk to one of us, you talk to all of us".

To become an effective service provider, the council needed root-and-branch reform: "When I first arrived it felt like 23,500 people against me" (chief executive). Forceful central leadership challenged entrenched vested interests and at the same time invested heavily in building and maintaining support for the changes among council members and staff. For example, staff now find out about important developments in letters from the chief executive sent to them at home rather than from the local paper and the unions. Meanwhile, senior managers have been empowered to make the required improvements happen: "We've given our directors more delegated power than has ever been seen in this city" (leader). By avoiding compulsory redundancies, headcount reductions of almost 2,000 have been achieved without industrial action.

Real service improvement is a long process and has been tackled in stages. Early on, external consultants underlined and amplified the messages in a damning OFSTED report. The threat of losing control of education to government-imposed management and privatisation forced unacceptable service standards to improve, with help from the IDeA: "Education was entirely command and control in the first six months, and then became deeply empowering" (chief executive). In the press release on OFSTED's re-inspection report, the Schools Minister said, "From being a failing authority 18 months ago, Liverpool are now delivering an effective education service…The progress that has been made shows that even the most disadvantaged education authorities can succeed with the right leadership."

Liverpool Direct has been created as a phone-based one-stop-shop for council services. With more than 125 staff, it is now Britain's largest local government call centre. It operates until 8.30pm and over weekends, with free red phones in libraries and other council buildings. Costs have been reduced and responsiveness improved by moving individual services into Liverpool Direct, in one example removing ten people from the decision chain that is triggered by the report of an abandoned vehicle. While the current focus is telephone-based, the council aims to integrate personal, telephone and electronic contact, and has plans to offer interactive web-based access as well as rolling out a programme of one-stop-shops throughout the city. To develop the information and communications technology systems needed to support the new council, IT staff are being transferred into a joint venture company managed by BT.

Impact: The transformation of the council is still in its early stages. Progress is fragile in some areas, and remains heavily dependent on a small group of key individuals. The partnership with BT carries the normal risks of major systems change and innovation. Not all front-line staff recognise the full scale of change taking place, nor sign up to the new vision. There are pockets of resistance where initial results – such as a rise from 20 per cent to 100 per cent of looked after children with an allocated social worker – may mask the fact that the old culture remains largely intact, along with traditional defensive behaviours and "bias for inaction". Dramatic organisational changes have not yet all been translated into service gains on the ground: "The PIs are our obsession. We actually track them monthly. We have reduced our staff, taken £65 million out of our cost base and yet the PIs are improving. It is a remarkable about-turn, but there's still a long way to go" (chief executive).

Critical factors

• Visible, committed and effective leadership, with a strong partnership between leading members and officers

• Delegation within a powerful overall vision

• Investment in communication

11. The current gap between expectations and delivery implies that, for many public service bodies, a step-change in performance is now required. 'Success' means achieving tangible improvements for customers through a change programme that leaves your organisation not depleted, demoralised and exhausted but energised, with its capabilities enhanced and the potential of its people freed up for the future. The challenge, then, is for step-change in performance to deliver improved results **and** a change-friendly organisation ready, willing and able to move into an ongoing cycle of continuous improvement.

KEY POINTS

Change management is one of the greatest challenges facing local public service leadership

- Change is not a simple, linear process, and sustained improvement is very difficult to achieve

- Incremental change is not sufficient to meet public and political expectations

- Organisations can use a step-change programme to build the capacity for continuous improvement

2. Role of the leadership team

Leading change

The four leadership roles

Key points

Leading change

12. Leadership is central to the quest for real and durable change. Public sector leadership is increasingly emerging as a topic of interest (see, for example, the recent Performance and Innovation Unit (PIU) research paper[I] which stresses that a clearer, shared understanding of what leadership behaviours work in delivering today's public services is fundamental to improved leadership). Concerns centre on a leadership deficit, due to a lack of leader development and the thanklessness (too many demands, too few resources, too little real control) of so many leadership roles, making it hard to attract and retain effective leaders in the public service. The public sector is not always perceived as an attractive career option. The PIU report suggests that this might be due partly to features of the operational environment that can act as barriers to good leadership, such as risk aversion, a blame culture, the lack of opportunities for reward and recognition, and the often unclear division of labour between politicians and officials. Perceptions about pay, conditions of work, progression and the value placed on the work may also contribute to the disincentives.

13. Change is one of the greatest demands on leadership, and evidence from public sector performance and the attitudes of staff underline the scale of the challenge [EXHIBIT 3, overleaf]. It was once the case that the leader (chief executive, managing director) of an organisation was expected to understand all the relevant technical areas encompassed by the 'business' and was thus able personally to develop strategy and make all key decisions. Those who reported to the leader exercised delegated management of the operational detail within their own functional areas. The days when that was an effective model are long gone. Leadership is increasingly a team as well as an individual challenge. Organisations are too complex and interdependent for one individual, however talented, to make all the decisions, even within a clear set of strategies defined by politicians. New structural forms, such as partnerships, are assuming increasing importance.

I   *Strengthening Leadership in the Public Sector*, Performance and Innovation Unit, 2001.

These involve leadership roles that extend beyond traditional organisational boundaries. And taking the perspective of the patient or user increasingly requires co-ordinated planning and decision making across several bodies within a locality. This growing complexity and interdependence affects the type of change that today's leaders are engaged in.

14. In local government, the distinction between political and managerial leadership and the relationship between them has become a major theme in its own right, particularly with the advent of new political governance structures. The emergence of the cabinet model has prompted a redefining of boundaries between political and managerial leadership. In the NHS, the relationship between clinical and managerial leaders, the establishment of clinical governance and the role of non-executives are all important factors affecting the management of change. Despite these different contexts, top managers seeking to bring about change in large and complex organisations face a common set of challenges. This paper aims to explore the challenges shared by the executive teams of local authorities, NHS trusts and a myriad of other big organisations.

15. The leadership of complex change demands a visible and committed top team. Your team is likely to focus on the chief executive and directors of a single organisation, or be made up of leaders from more than one body working together to bring about cross-cutting change. Either way, the principles of change leadership and management remain very much the same. You need to be more than a group of disparate individuals with specific functional roles, but rather a genuine team with a shared sense of purpose and collective responsibility for delivering the end goals [CASE STUDY 3, overleaf]

EXHIBIT 3   ATTITUDES TO CHANGE AMONG LOCAL STAFF

While nearly three-quarters of staff understand the need for change, less than one-quarter think it is well managed.

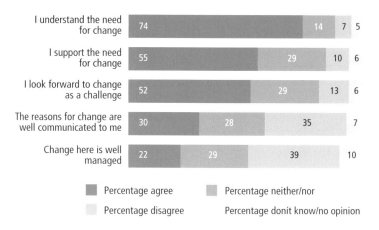

I understand the need for change	74	14	7	5
I support the need for change	55	29	10	6
I look forward to change as a challenge	52	29	13	6
The reasons for change are well communicated to me	30	28	35	7
Change here is well managed	22	29	39	10

■ Percentage agree   ■ Percentage neither/nor
■ Percentage disagree   ■ Percentage don't know/no opinion

Source: MORI (Sharing A Vision, 2000) Question: To what extent do you agree or disagree with the following statements?

CASE STUDY 3   SIGNALLING CHANGE ON ALL FRONTS

Background: The London Borough of Barking and Dagenham (LBB&D) is changing from a paternalistic, traditional authority into a modern London borough that is actively seeking to improve. External challenges have helped to drive change, through the introduction of best value and a highly critical review of LBB&D social services, which placed them under special monitoring. The borough is now working to overcome a culture of poor cross-directorate working by members and officers, and low levels of public involvement in service development and implementation.

Approach: The 1997 local and general elections saw the council leader come to the end of his term and the chief executive announce his retirement. Up to this point, both political and organisational leadership had been characterised by inertia, and LBB&D had found it very difficult to initiate significant change. Convincing members, staff at all levels of the borough and the wider community of the need to change has been a theme of LBB&D's progress so far.

Members and officers were keen to adopt the modernisation agenda for public services, and to respond to external challenges, but lacked a vision for a modern LBB&D. In the leadership gap, senior officers managed themselves, reshaping the top team and taking turns to chair. They focused on developing new corporate priorities and engaging the support of members for wide-ranging changes, beginning with modernising the way that the borough is managed. Officers have worked to establish new relationships with members, such as through a series of workshops to develop community priorities using an external consultant, and Saturday briefings to keep them abreast of best value developments.

Acting on the challenges provided by best value, LBB&D has made a good start towards developing meaningful, community-wide consultation:

- The findings of a borough-wide community survey signalled the need for change and were used by members and officers in workshops to help to shape corporate aims and match them to the community's experience.

- In 2000, Barking and Dagenham citizens' panel was established by MORI on behalf of the authority. The panel of 1,000 residents was selected to represent a cross-section of the community. It was consulted on last year's performance plan and the borough's draft community priorities, and has provided comments on a range of services so far.

- Six community forums have been established, providing ongoing feedback about the types of change they want from the borough. Officers and councillors discuss detailed issues as residents raise them. The community forums have now been given some decision-making powers on budgets, so that they can select and fund projects in their local areas.

LBB&D's new chief executive sees his role as promoting and sustaining the impetus for change, developing and communicating a shared sense of direction. Under his lead, LBB&D takes reputation management seriously and actively seeks external awards and recognition to signal confidence in its progress. Badging the change programme as 'Barking and Dagenham 2000' has raised its profile and sent clear signals across the authority that LBB&D was determined to improve. Monthly newsletters were issued to all personnel, and the borough used the title for formal 'Barking and Dagenham 2000' briefing days for all staff, with professional audiovisual support and polished presentations to communicate the change programme and reinforce the fact that it is now doing things differently.

The borough expects staff to develop in line with the new ethos, and has revised its staff performance management system accordingly. The chief executive published his own objectives within the authority, showing his accountability and demonstrating the links between personal and corporate objectives. Competency assessment was established for the senior team and the process is now cascading through the organisation, with some staff leaving as a result. LBB&D is considering new ways to present itself as an attractive and competitive employer. The borough is now developing a balanced scorecard as a method of translating the corporate objectives into service targets and actions to improve local service delivery.

Impact: An IDeA peer review in March 2000 recognised the progress that the borough has made in modernising. A recent best value inspection of political and community leadership has reported that LBB&D's performance is fair and will probably improve significantly in the short term. It found that corporate aims were owned by the council's political leadership and senior management team. It also reported that LBB&D had made a positive start to improving communications with the public. A recent survey showed that 70 per cent of tenants believed the borough took their views into consideration when making decisions. The borough was also shortlisted for two *Local Government Chronicle* awards. Between 1997 and 2000, education in the borough was the fastest improving in the country for Key Stage 2. In April 2001, special monitoring was lifted from social services.

The leadership team at LBB&D recognises that changing the culture of a whole borough will take much more time, and that progress is still fragile. The leadership team is also aware that work needs to be done to improve the borough's performance on equalities issues, and this is now at the heart of the borough's programme for change. Non-executive members must also understand their role in the modernised borough and councillors should actively challenge its performance and progress.

Critical factors

* Leadership team signalling the need for change at every opportunity

* Making use of external pressure and engaging members to create momentum for change

16. As the leadership team in an environment that is constantly generating new demands, change is part of your daily lives. Guiding the organisation through a change programme, your collective aim is to deliver tangible results and, in doing so, to create a change-friendly organisation that is capable of continuous performance improvement. To do this, you need, as a team, to have a common understanding of the change process and of your leadership role within it.

The four leadership roles

17. We have defined change leadership as a team responsibility. Leadership teams are made up of individuals who have different leadership styles. There is no single model of leadership style that is needed to deliver change successfully. However, we have defined a core set of leadership roles that are particularly important for steering through change. They can be grouped into four areas, which together constitute transformational leadership [EXHIBIT 4, overleaf]. The emphasis on each area varies through the different phases of a major change programme (see section 'Sustaining focus on the key priorities', page 52).

EXHIBIT 4   FOUR KEY DIMENSIONS NEEDED TO LEAD CHANGE

The emphasis on each leadership role varies through the different stages of a major change programme.

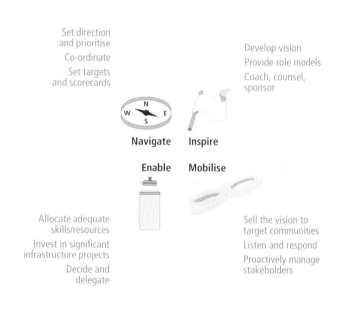

Set direction
and prioritise
Co-ordinate
Set targets
and scorecards

Develop vision
Provide role models
Coach, counsel,
sponsor

Navigate   Inspire

Enable   Mobilise

Allocate adequate
skills/resources
Invest in significant
infrastructure projects
Decide and
delegate

Sell the vision to
target communities
Listen and respond
Proactively manage
stakeholders

Source: Audit Commission adaptation of Accenture

18. The four change leadership roles are:

Inspire

• Develop a shared vision that people inside the organisation and its major external stakeholders can buy into and endorse. Achieving this will clearly be highly dependent on the nature of the organisation – in a local council it will happen in a very different way than, for example, in a police force. The more that the vision has been developed in an explicitly inclusive way, the easier it will be to convince others to support it.

- Act as role models for the organisation; for example, in the emphasis that you place on listening to customers and in the way you treat your staff. Top team behaviour sends powerful signals, both positive and negative. Behaviour that runs counter to the vision will be noticed and can seriously undermine the culture that you are trying to establish. For example, firing a senior manager for a single adverse event that reached the press while failing to react to time and budget overruns on a major corporate project sends a strong message about what your organisation regards as important. Your attitude to managed risk-taking and the way you react when things go wrong have a profound influence on behaviour at all levels of your organisation.

- Finally, you will need to develop the next generation of leaders by coaching, counselling and sponsoring talented individuals at all levels of the organisation. Big change programmes tend to cut across traditional hierarchies and provide valuable opportunities for less senior staff to take on leadership roles as part of their development.

Mobilise

- Communicate the vision to staff and stakeholders to build support for the change programme. It is important to have a clear picture of the key interests whose support you need; this could include councillors and non-executives, staff in your own organisation, unions, partner bodies, users, the community you serve and specific groups within it. You will need to identify the most important groups and individuals in relation to your own change programme to develop a robust communication strategy, and have a good grip of the communication function to ensure that the messages are delivered to the right audiences in the appropriate way.

- Reassure significant stakeholders that their voices are being heard [CASE STUDY 4, overleaf] It is valuable to have an understanding of their concerns and to involve them as far as possible in the change, at the very least providing ongoing feedback where a meaningful dialogue is impossible.

Background: From 1998 onwards, NHS modernisation has required Bradford, as elsewhere, to form stable and functioning primary care groups (PCGs) and, in time, primary care trusts (PCTs), that meet the specific healthcare needs of local people and improve local health.

Approach: In 1998, Bradford Health Authority (BHA) divided up the Bradford area based around viable population sizes for new PCGs, and proposed a configuration of four PCG/Ts that created all-new boundaries. The new Bradford South and West PCG/T of around 150,000 people had no 'natural' geographical focus or sense of cohesion. It required the merger of three fund-holding consortia with little shared history or established co-operative working, and some local GPs were hostile to the change.

The PCG chair (and subsequent PCT chief executive) and board sought the support of all clinicians, plus local community and voluntary workers, as the commitment of all stakeholders was key to successful change.

The board recognised that it was not enough to overcome GP resistance, even though this in itself was a challenge: all stakeholders had to accept the PCG/T as the focus of future primary care services, and build a shared sense of identity and a commitment to the new organisation.

This became the early priority of the PCG/T board. It devoted huge personal attention and energy to building relationships with clinicians and the local community. Board members listened closely to what was happening on the ground, maintained a high profile around practices and made sure that they were accessible to all GPs, intervening directly to deal with local problems or rumblings of concern about the planned changes.

Given the disparate group of stakeholders, the PCG/T recognised the need for consistent messages and clear, up-to-the-minute internal communications within the PCG board and management team, and with all stakeholders. Regular, purposeful meetings with GP-leads and allocated time for every practice to discuss the changes helped clinicians feel that they owned and were driving local strategy: "What really achieved results was the sense of identity among all stakeholders that the PCT was theirs and they could shape its development" (PCT chief executive).

BHA acts as enabler for the change, monitoring progress with a light touch as long as the PCT delivers excellent performance, but making it clear to PCT managers that they should expect much closer attention should performance slip.

Impact: By securing GP involvement, Bradford South and West PCT has made significant developments in local services:

- GPs carry out a range of specialist procedures including minor operations, diagnostics and triage of out-patient referrals. This ensures that patients meet with consultants with all supporting test results ready and shortens the time to treatment;

- specialist primary care services look after people with diabetes and identify, then care for, people with early signs of coronary heart disease; and

- practices promote well-being and tackle the causes of ill-health, for example using lifestyle assessments and prescribing programmes of health and fitness.

The GP specialist scheme has carried out 6,000 procedures and 9,000 out-patient appointments, helping the PCT (and the HA) achieve their waiting times and list targets. The PCT has received national recognition for its work so far and is a beacon site for implementing GP specialisms. The Secretary of State for Health has praised its approach to health promotion, saying: "What we are seeing here in Bradford is practically what we would like to see across the country..."

Critical factors

- Focusing energy on key stakeholders
- Establishing a high profile presence and intervening personally when needed
- Building consensus by communicating clearly and honestly
- Understanding what motivates key stakeholders to harness their support
- Allocating time for stakeholder involvement in debate and discussion

- Focus and prioritise to deliver a successful change programme. This will inevitably mean reducing the emphasis on some areas that are seen as important (see section 'Sustaining focus on the key priorities', page 52). This re-prioritisation needs to be explained to, and understood by, your key stakeholders. Local leaders are required to find a balance between legitimate national priorities and specific local needs. Best value provides a framework to support this prioritisation through a council's best value performance plan and the programme of best value reviews. Implementing local public service agreements will place further focus on priorities for performance improvement in key areas agreed between local and central government. In the climate of initiative overload in the NHS, careful communication is needed to build understanding and buy-in from regional offices for the priorities that you have set. External stakeholders will want reassurance that your approach will deliver tangible gains in a realistic time period and will lay the groundwork for broader improvement after the first wave of changes have come through.

Enable

- Create space and find resources. This means making tough and well-informed choices about where money can be found. Having control over the finance function is critical to ensuring that resources and policy run hand in hand, as they should. Picking individuals with the right skills to lead the change process is also key. Deciding how to resource the programme always involves tensions and dilemmas. The problem is knowing how to balance the need to keep the show on the road – continuing to deliver adequate services day-to-day – while freeing up sufficient time and resources to invest in the change programme. Inevitably, the staff you would most like to have leading the change are the very people who are most difficult to spare from their day jobs. Typically, such capable individuals hold key roles and already carry an unreasonable workload. Releasing able staff is only possible where departments are prepared to shoulder the extra burden, and where a sense of excitement encourages staff to risk investing their energy in something uncertain. This is yet another reason why the active support of the senior team is so essential.

- Recognise and accept that change requires flexibility of people and investment. Part of the leadership role is actively reprioritising and negotiating to find the critical resources when they are needed. In the modern environment, it is difficult to envisage any major change that does not, at some stage, require investment in infrastructure projects, particularly information technology. The other support functions that are likely to be stretched are in the human resources area, as changes affect the kinds of people you need, the roles and skills that are required, the way that people work and how they are assessed and rewarded. As changes affect jobs and terms and conditions, a proactive approach to industrial relations is essential.

- Make the key decisions quickly. It is deeply disempowering to work in an organisation where there is no clear decision making or sense of urgency or purpose for improvement. The organisation will be able to deliver against the vision only if key decisions are made speedily and project managers are given delegated authority to move things forward.

Navigate

- Set the course for change and translate the vision into a manageable programme. This requires ruthless prioritisation so that the organisation is able to focus scarce resources on the things that are needed to deliver service improvements.

- Co-ordinate the change programme through the top team as a whole or a sub-group that is more involved in the mechanics of the programme. The purpose of co-ordination is to keep the whole programme on track, monitor progress and manage the trade-offs and dependencies between different component projects with good information and a light touch.

- Set targets and monitor performance. Your over-arching vision is not useful as a management tool until it is translated into concrete targets. By setting the overall targets you determine the direction of the programme as a whole. By monitoring performance you can keep track of your progress. Targets may be a combination of process, output and outcome measures, but extended timescales for implementation mean that intermediate indicators will be needed if you are to be sure that you are moving forward as planned. Navigation needs to be an ongoing activity – setting the course once and defaulting to automatic pilot will not keep the vessel on course through the uncharted waters of change. Checking the readings and recalibrating measures and targets is necessary throughout the journey to make sure that gains are sustained, that measures remain relevant and that targets continue to be appropriately stretching.

KEY POINTS

Effective leadership is key to delivering change

- Leadership is increasingly a team as well as an individual responsibility

- Leaders must understand the process of change in order to guide their organisations through the change journey

- Leadership styles vary, but a core set of change leadership roles can be defined
  - develop and promote a shared vision
  - mobilise staff and stakeholder support
  - make key decisions and navigate through the change journey
  - support the organisation to deliver

3. Local ownership

Building support for change

The role of good practice

Communication

Key points

Building support for change

19. Directive change is possible, and can deliver impressive results in certain circumstances, as discussed in the introductory section and illustrated in case study 9 (the National Literacy Strategy), page 54. But for organic or transformational change, some degree of local ownership is imperative. It is also an essential building block for organisations seeking to develop a capacity for ongoing improvement [CASE STUDY 5]

CASE STUDY 5   RESHAPING SERVICES TO HELP OLDER PEOPLE TO LIVE INDEPENDENTLY

Background: Older people needing help and support would rather be in their own homes than in hospital or residential care. The challenge for Dudley Social Services staff was to turn a largely residential care-based service into one that helped people to cope at home.

Approach: Meeting clients' aspirations required profound changes to the way that services were delivered and the role of social services staff. Senior managers shared a vision of home-based care with operational staff, who turned it into clear objectives. They were challenged and supported by an Audit Commission report.[I] Using it as a benchmark for local progress, staff report that "it helped us to ask the right questions" about where money was spent, what skills were needed, and how they might work with other local partners in providing care.

Creating a residential rehabilitation service was an important part of the vision. It provides care for up to five weeks, building confidence and re-establishing the skills that older people need to manage successfully around the home, such as basic cooking and using equipment for personal care. Careful assessment and care planning are used to set goals with clients based on their specific needs and priorities. A team that believed in changing the ways it worked with older people led a pilot scheme, building relationships with stakeholders – GPs and other community services, hospitals, and private residential care homes – who, working together, form the network of support needed for viable home-based care.

I   *The Coming of Age: Improving Care Services for Elderly People,*
Audit Commission, 1997.

Senior managers invested their time as influential 'champions', promoting the service locally and within the wider authority.

Impact: The new residential rehabilitation service has proved highly effective in enabling people to stay in their own homes, where previously permanent residential care might have been the only option. Clients are very satisfied. Monitoring and evaluation were built in so that staff in social services can learn from user feedback and the experiences of similar services elsewhere. This will enable the service to continue to develop and improve.

Critical factors

*   Clear senior management vision, communicated well to staff and the community
*   Opportunity for enthusiastic staff to shape and test changes in the local context to build wider commitment
*   Senior management support for operational staff implementing the changes
*   Ongoing monitoring and feedback from clients

20. Not every employee has to be deeply committed to the vision for change to succeed. But the majority of stakeholders and staff must accept the need for change and support the leadership's direction of travel. In a large organisation, only a fraction of people affected by a change programme can be architects, but a much broader group can be engaged and involved in other ways [CASE STUDY 6]

LOCAL OWNERSHIP DRIVING A SERIES OF IMPROVEMENTS   CASE STUDY 6

Background: Ophthalmology at the Oxford Radcliffe Hospitals NHS Trust is a high volume service, treating around 5,000 in-patients annually and providing 44,000 out-patient appointments. Waiting lists for eye surgery had been rising since October 1997, and by March 1998 there were 2,250 patients waiting for surgery. Additional funding to target waiting lists was applied to rectify what was initially seen as a simple problem.

Approach: A multi-professional team, consisting of the lead consultant, senior nurse, directorate manager and trust waiting list officer focused on reducing the growing waiting lists for cataract operations.

They calculated that increased theatre capacity was needed and, as a temporary measure, held additional twilight operating sessions to clear the backlog. Introducing telephone pre-assessment of selected patients and a waiting area inside theatres helped to reduce time between operations and enabled more people to be treated. One year on, lists had fallen by 13 per cent.

However, removing the bottleneck in in-patient activity caused the workload for out-patient services to grow dramatically, increasing activity overall by about 20 per cent. The review group therefore extended the programme to cover all components of the ophthalmology service. They systematically analysed the patient journey, from receipt of a GP referral letter through to the end of treatment. The group was struck by the interdependency of services, how many different staff groups were involved in the patient pathway, and how little patients' needs featured in the process.

Their analysis challenged long-standing practices, and involved local staff in generating solutions for improvement. Staff identified making better use of doctors' time at out-patient clinics as critical to removing the new bottlenecks. Having quantified demand, other staff were able to support doctors better by implementing some 'quick fixes', such as:

- booking appointments to match the medical staff available for each clinic;

- agreeing appointment times in advance with patients, to help reduce non-attendances;

- enabling patients to wait closer to consulting rooms; and

- having notes to hand in waiting areas.

To manage the increased workload for the whole out-patient service, doctors introduced Saturday morning clinics and took an active part in developing new targets and in monitoring progress.

Impact: Sustaining efficiency gains has proved difficult, but overall in-patient activity has increased by 3.4 per cent and the waiting list has fallen by 10 per cent (over 200 people).

Staff involvement in improving services has rippled outwards and led to further benefits for patients. For example, analysing the patient pathway revealed that staff in other departments, such as accident and emergency, spent a lot of time directing ophthalmology patients around the hospital. As a result, signposting has been improved.

Change is spreading beyond the hospital setting and now involves primary care and community ophthalmology. Ongoing analysis of workload and activity is generating new ideas to improve the efficiency and quality of the patient experience, such as direct referral from community to hospital.

In 1999, the service was awarded beacon status for its waiting list initiative.

Critical factors

- Key staff led the change process, using their expertise and knowledge to identify solutions and build support for change
- Change was built on a systematic analysis of bottlenecks in the service, using activity data and a review of the patient pathway through care

21. Building support for change is a huge challenge for the leadership team. Commitment is particularly difficult to engender where powerful interest groups use a professional code to resist the direction of change and, at the opposite extreme, where the people affected have no meaningful involvement in decision making and where key issues are decided far from the front line. Command-and-control cultures may hold superficial appeal when it comes to driving through change. But it is often precisely where individuals feel disempowered and distant from decision making that change is resisted most successfully. Conversely, autonomy and delegated decision making can be powerful allies of change. They enable the people closest to customers to respond to changes in the environment and better meet the needs of individuals and communities [CASE STUDY 7, overleaf]

Background: In 1996, an Audit Commission report[1] used fieldwork across England and Wales, questionnaires from local education authorities (LEAs) and a survey of parents, to highlight the mismatch between pupil numbers and the number of school places. This mismatch was wasting resources where places were unfilled, and causing large classes and overcrowding where more provision was needed.

Approach: The analysis showed how local improvement was being blocked by a 'policy gridlock' of conflicting messages from central government. The report suggested a clear way out of 'gridlock' and became a powerful lever for change. Policymakers responded swiftly by making LEAs accountable for supply and allocation and empowered them to plan for and manage school places. Subsequent policy changes, first highlighted in the report, include:

- targeted monitoring of school rolls, with a focus on any school with less than 75 per cent of places filled. A school may provide a sound case for staying open, such as geographical factors or the likelihood of a failing school improving. If it cannot, the LEA has the power to close it and redistribute resources more efficiently;

- school organisation plans where each LEA, in partnership with school governors and other key local stakeholders, sets out its forecast of how it intends to deal with the supply and demand for school places over a five-year period;

- asset management plans, which support more local decision making on the allocation of funding for capital improvements; and

- a new code of practice on school admissions, which ensures that parents receive better and more consistent information.

Impact: Since 1997, surplus school places have fallen by 64,000.

Critical factors
- Objective evidence of the need for change
- Empowering localities to plan and manage their own resources

---

[1] *Trading Places: The Supply and Allocation of School Places*, Audit Commission, 1996.

The role of good practice

22. In the transformational model, successful strategies for change combine committed and visible leadership ("There is no alternative to change") with the maximum degree of engagement and involvement by staff and users. This still applies when adopting good practice that has been successful elsewhere. The Audit Commission has always stressed the need to tailor solutions to local circumstances. There are many sources of good practice – including networks, beacons, conferences, publications and databases – some of which provide opportunities for continuing contact with other organisations for ongoing learning. Whatever the source of good practice, the learning from our research is clear: you cannot expect simply to import someone else's good practice into your own organisation. It is necessary to re-examine, if not reinvent, the wheel, building on what other people have discovered. There are two main reasons:

- **The wrong solution:** modern organisations are complex organisms, each made up of specific individuals and with their own particular heritage, existing within a unique network of relationships with customers, stakeholders and other bodies operating together in the local environment. No externally generated blueprint is likely to be sensitive enough to accommodate this unique set of conditions, so the detailed template must be developed locally.

- **The right solution, not fully adopted:** if you want people to change their behaviour in any other way than following a simple, easily enforceable set of rules, they need to invest in the changes you are asking them to make. They need to be convinced of the benefits both conceptually (this is good for customers and for the organisation) and personally (this is good for me/ my family/ my job satisfaction/ my career/ the rewards available to me) [BOX A]

BOX A: ASSESSING GOOD PRACTICE

"Don't reinvent the wheel" is a familiar message. The successes and failures of others offer useful lessons, but what works in one situation won't necessarily work in another. Involving your staff in modifying any ideas and practices taken from other organisations to suit your circumstances is key to building local ownership.

Operational staff are well placed to:

• provide a realistic assessment of your present situation; where you are now and where you want to be, and the local context, including the resources available;

• assess good practice ideas from other organisations by asking:
  – What exactly are they doing?
  – Does it really work? What is the evidence for their claims of success?
  – Why does it work? What elements are critical to success both in terms of the circumstances and in the mechanisms used?; and

• assess how it might best be applied to your situation:
  – What differences in the local context either require changes in the mechanisms used or affect the prospects of success?
  – How might the mechanisms be adapted to suit the local context?
  – Would it then still be cost-effective, and what needs to be tested to establish this?

They may want to pilot or experiment with ideas before introducing them across the organisation. Your role is to make the high-level decisions and provide the support and resources that operational staff need to develop, test and implement the chosen approach.

Source: Audit Commission

23. To adopt solutions that will work, stakeholders must believe in them enough to make them real. The key to this is for them, or people whom they feel represent them such as unions, peers or user groups, to have had a say in how things should change. Both organisations and individuals can evolve sophisticated strategies for resisting and subverting change, even while superficially appearing to accept it. This is not to say that resistance to change can never be overcome, but self-generated change has a much better chance of taking root and delivering sustained improvements in performance [EXHIBIT 5].

Involving stakeholders in a change programme increases the chance of sustained improvement.

IMPOSITION	Outright hostility	Token compliance	Grudging acceptance	Lukewarm enthusiasm	Real commitment	INVOLVEMENT
	Refusal Resignation Industrial action	Lip-service to new ideas Subversion	Comply only where immediate benefit evident	Momentum stalled by obstacles	Enthusiastic/ evangelical Willing to take risks Persistent in the face of barriers	

Depth and durability of change achieved

Low   High

Source: Audit Commission

Communication

24. Designing meaningful stakeholder involvement into your change programme is not a trivial task. Differential levels of engagement are appropriate for different groups. There will typically be a core of highly involved members (for local government), senior managers, clinicians (in the NHS) and other staff who are central to shaping and driving the programme forward. This core group will probably grow as the change programme progresses and more people are drawn into it. Beyond the core group, it is useful to develop a fairly comprehensive plan for timely, purposeful, two-way communication with key stakeholders throughout the stages of the programme, using a variety of different formats, channels and methods.

25. This is best done in a systematic way, breaking down the priority audiences into groupings by type (including staff, unions, customers, community, other external stakeholders), role and level within your own staff (recognising the legitimately differing communication needs

Local ownership

Communication

of managers, front-line and support staff, for example) and geographical location. Against each group, the communication objectives and activities can be mapped out over time to ensure an ongoing flow of information and contact that enables you to reach out to and influence key audiences and keeps them informed and involved [CASE STUDY 8]

CASE STUDY 8   TARGETING KEY AUDIENCES TO BUILD SUPPORT FOR CHANGE

Background: In October 1996, The Ridings in Halifax achieved national notoriety as discipline broke down completely during an OFSTED inspection. It was labelled a failing school with miserable academic results and endemic truancy and discipline problems, and placed in special measures with an acting headteacher and associate head seconded in from other local schools.

Approach: The Ridings turnaround strategy was based on establishing a clear vision for the school – to give pupils the best opportunity to fulfil their potential by maximising the quality of teaching and learning – and engaging the support of four key groups to deliver it.

• Headteacher and **staff** together revisited the school's existing aims and objectives to build a shared set of values and aspirations that guided every individual change, from the timetable to praise letters, from lunchtime to uniform and from the length of the school day to rewards for good behaviour. For the first six months, quality of teaching was agreed as the key priority and a tough but transparent performance management system introduced to back it up. At a critical, high risk staff meeting, formal classroom observation was accepted, along with re-establishing management structures, and clarifying the roles and responsibilities of every individual member of staff.

• The **governing body** at The Ridings had been severely criticised by OFSTED, but through the appointment of some new members and with active encouragement from the headteacher and her team, governors were involved and engaged with the changes taking place at the school.

• The support and commitment of **pupils** was harnessed by responding to their concerns, providing the stability and reassurance they were seeking and moving from a negative, blame culture to one of positive reinforcement, where opportunities for praise were actively sought out. The approach to dealing with low attendance was based around changing what was on offer in the school, particularly for children with special educational needs, to attract truants back into the classroom.

• Having expressed their anger and frustration at past failure, **parents** were involved as part of the solution. A regular newsletter was established and parents were invited to the praise assemblies that recognised pupils' progress and achievements. Changes in response to parents' views clearly demonstrated that their voices were being heard. These included making parents' evenings much more welcoming and holding meetings of the re-established PTA in the pub, where many parents felt more comfortable than in school.

Impact: The Ridings is now judged by OFSTED to be a good and improving school, where constant attention to the quality of teaching is reaping its rewards, as evidenced by progress against many key performance measures.

Critical factors

• Shared vision

• Managed approach to engaging key stakeholders

26. MORI research in the public sector shows that staff who feel they are kept well informed are twice as likely to:

• feel involved with their organisation; and

• understand its objectives.

They are also over twice as likely to:

• recognise clear goals;

• feel secure in their job; and

• feel that they can make the best use of their skills and abilities.

Good communication is one of the most powerful mechanisms to help leadership teams to build understanding and support to deliver change successfully. These days, communications thinking is well advanced and an enormous variety of options are readily available.

Techniques for community consultation are described in an Audit Commission management paper.[l]

27. It is hard to overstate the amount of senior time and energy that it takes to communicate a major change programme. Listening to leaders who have transformed their organisations, this is frequently cited as a key learning point because, when it comes to communicating about change, many commonsense assumptions turn out to be wrong [EXHIBIT 6]. Communication begins with convincing people of the need to change. Your leadership team needs a powerful rationale for change that chimes with the organisation's own value system – its view of why it exists and what it needs to do. The rationale needs to be persuasively articulated and repeatedly reinforced in a simple way, using language and symbols that people understand and identify with. Investment in communication is needed throughout the change journey.

EXHIBIT 6   COMMON COMMUNICATION MYTHS

Many commonsense assumptions about communicating change are mistaken.

We must wait until we have all the answers before we communicate

We haven't said anything yet so we aren't communicating

We only need to communicate with the people who are directly involved

There's nothing new to say so we don't need to communicate now

It's complicated and could be alarming if it's misinterpreted, so we'd better say nothing

We've covered this before so we don't need to say it again

It's taken us months to work this out, but you'll understand it after one presentation/leaflet/conversation

Our job is to make the information available; anyone who's interested will come and find it

Source: Audit Commission adaptation of Jeanie Daniel Duck

l   *Listen Up: Effective Community Consultation*, Audit Commission, 1999.

28. For communication to be effective, the channels must meet the needs of the audience. Research shows that staff have strong views about what kinds of communication they prefer and trust. It is hardly surprising that they deeply dislike hearing news about their work that directly affects them through the local media or the rumour mill. Team briefings and face-to-face contact with line managers are the two most favoured approaches. This highlights the need for an effective cascade briefing system so that important messages about the change programme can be quickly and accurately disseminated throughout the organisation in the way that people prefer. Different sorts of mechanisms are needed to pick up staff views and feed them into the change programme [EXHIBITS 7 AND 8, overleaf].

HOW STAFF RECEIVE INFORMATION AND THEIR PREFERENCES   EXHIBIT 7

Staff prefer face-to-face communication with colleagues.

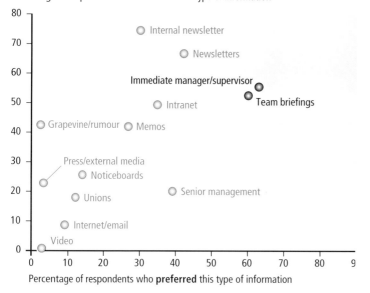

Source: MORI (Sharing A Vision, 2000) Question: Here is a list of ways of getting information. How do you receive information and how would you prefer to receive information?

EXHIBIT 8   HOW MUCH STAFF TRUST DIFFERENT SOURCES OF INFORMATION

Team meetings are the most trusted form of communication.

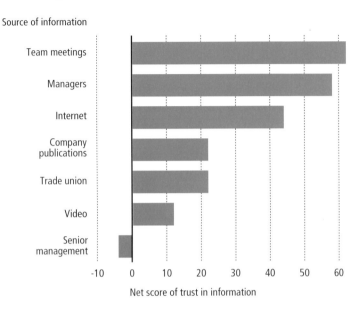

Source of information

Source: MORI (Sharing A Vision, 2000) Question: To what extent do you trust the following sources of information? -2=not at all, +2=total trust.
Base: All working who expressed a view (net score).

29. Large-scale change is rarely possible without casualties. Whatever mechanisms are used, the leadership team is ultimately responsible for seeing that the negative effects on individuals are handled in a fair and professional way, respecting the rights and dignity of those who must go and managing the impact on those who stay. Maintaining motivation and performance under these circumstances is extremely taxing, and line managers who are directly affected are likely to need extra support leading up to, during and after any restructuring takes place.

Local ownership

Communication

KEY POINTS

Building support for change is essential for continuous improvement in a changing world

- Imposed change tends to be resisted over the long term
- Each organisation is complex and unique, so good practice is best handled with care
- Communication is a critical activity to build buy-in

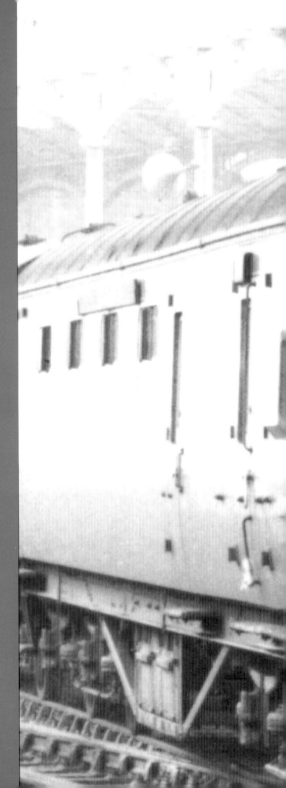

4. Sustaining focus on the key priorities

Doing less to achieve more

The change curve

Key points

Doing less to achieve more

30. The necessity of sticking to a small number of key priorities in order to achieve deep and durable change is illustrated well by the National Literacy Strategy [CASE STUDY 9]

CASE STUDY 9   SUSTAINED FOCUS ON A CLEAR OBJECTIVE

Background: National tests of pupils during the 1990s showed that attainment in literacy throughout England was unacceptably low. Fewer than 50 per cent of pupils at age 11 met national expectations in writing. Standards of adult literacy continued to cause concern, and national and international studies indicated that one in five adults had poor literacy skills, placing England near the bottom of the European league table. Variable pupil performance across local education authorities (LEAs), sometimes confounding expectations based on socio-economic factors, encouraged the view that with consistently high quality input there could be a levelling up of performance.

Approach: The DfEE employed a national team of key practitioners in literacy education to devise a strategy that:

- identified the most effective teaching practices nationally and internationally;

- provided a detailed blueprint for the skills and knowledge that should be taught to all pupils from five to eleven years;

- disseminated key teaching practices to teachers through a centrally driven professional development programme, managed through LEAs; and

- set clear expectations for daily teaching practices.

In September 1998, the strategy was introduced to all primary and special schools, with comprehensive training modules reflecting key teaching practices. Professional development programmes were produced centrally and rolled out by literacy consultants, funded by the DfEE and LEAs, to teachers in the lowest attaining 40 per cent of schools. All schools received central funding for resources to implement the recommended practices.

Impact: Despite early resistance from teachers, headteachers and academics, almost every school in England has adopted the strategy. Qualitative evidence suggests that pupils and teachers have increased motivation and subject knowledge. In the last two years, standards nationally have risen by 10 per cent for 11 year olds and it seems likely that the programme will meet its target set for 2002. All but a small percentage of LEAs have shown significant improvements in pupil performance, particularly in reading. The rigorous programme of professional development has given teachers a shared language to discuss approaches to teaching literacy.

Central funding continues, but the focus has moved to increased local ownership. Teachers will be encouraged to build on the national programme to enable the strategy to evolve and deliver further improvements in literacy standards.

Critical factors

The National Literacy Strategy shows how a highly directive approach can be successful where there is:

- a recognised need for step-change, starting from a low performance base;
- good understanding of what works, supported by strong research evidence;
- sustained focus on clear, quantifiable goals backed up by substantial investment;
- close monitoring; and
- focus on a single sector, with limited interdependencies.

31. It is widely understood that organisations that attempt simultaneously to pursue a number of unconnected strategies are unlikely to succeed with any one of them. But in the real world of multiple objectives and competing public sector priorities, defining and sticking to a limited set of core goals is a major challenge [CASE STUDY 10, overleaf]. Relentless focus on essentials is easier when organisational survival is at stake, less so when there are many areas that need improving but the overall situation is not in itself perilous. Without a clear sense of strategic direction, the odds are stacked against any major change programme.

32. In local government, the strategic vision should emerge as a result of the local democratic process, for which there is no direct local equivalent in the NHS, police or fire services. New political structures and the introduction of the cabinet system will also have an impact. But in any local body, the executive team has a key role in translating overall vision into a manageable programme whose constituent projects can be delegated to teams within the organisation, and overall progress and outcomes planned, monitored and measured. This programme must, first and foremost, be owned by the top team, so that when facing difficult decisions about where scarce resources and management attention should be invested, there is consensus about protecting what is necessary to deliver the change programme.

33. The need for the change programme to have the support of key stakeholders, both internal and external has been described in earlier sections. This support provides a vital buffer against the latest urgent pressure or political enthusiasm, whether generated centrally or locally. Proactively selling your vision is a necessary investment to create the space for you as the local leadership team to pursue your goals in the face of diversion and distraction. This probably involves explicit handling strategies for the most influential people and groups. A well-articulated vision, even a broad-brush one, that stakeholders support, and which is seen to be delivering results in improved services, is the most effective defence against the danger of new priorities being imposed from outside.

CASE STUDY 10   FOCUSING ON CORE PRIORITIES

Background: In 1998, Birmingham City Council Education Welfare Service (EWS) was criticised by OFSTED as being too broad-based rather than concentrating on the areas that mattered most; improving attendance and reducing school exclusions. These messages were echoed by the EWS's own consultation with headteachers.

Approach: The external auditor helped the service to develop an action plan to sharpen its focus on core business and maximise EWS's time spent working in partnership with schools. The plan included:

- clearly defining how the service works with schools, including criteria for involvement in individual cases and setting standards;

- reducing the range of functions covered by the service, limiting involvement in issues other than attendance (such as supporting parents of excluded pupils); and

- using qualified staff more selectively. Administrative staff took over tasks such as hardship applications and finding school places, freeing up education social workers' time for attendance issues.

The management and structure of the service were revised to support these changes, with increased accountability for all staff and improved reporting mechanisms. A communications programme was set up to explain the rationale for change and build staff support.

Outcomes are now closely tracked so that the service can identify needs and problem areas more efficiently and allocate appropriate resources. Individual school plans are used to monitor effectiveness against agreed standards and provide regular feedback and direct support to schools. The service has also developed a good practice guide on improving and maintaining pupil attendance, which has been well received by schools.

Impact: A follow-up review by the auditor in 2000 showed that while absence rates are still above the national average, they have improved, and faster than the national rate, without any increase in cost. The proportion of resources directed towards key areas has increased and education social workers now devote an additional 10 per cent of their time direct to schools. The annual survey of schools shows increased satisfaction with the service.

The next challenge is to build on this progress and strengthen the performance management framework. This will be informed by the service's best value review, active collaboration with comparator LEAs, and an action plan developed from the auditor's review.

Critical factors

- Clear picture of core priorities, communicated well to staff
- Sustained focus and close tracking of what matters to users

Doing less to achieve more

The change curve

34. Persistence, resilience and consistency of purpose are essential for delivering a significant change programme. The 'change curve' developed by Jeanie Duck,[1] neatly illustrates why this is so. The change curve describes five stages that organisations typically go through in a successful major change journey. It is possible to subjectively plot the organisation's morale and confidence as it progresses through the five stages, producing a characteristic irregular curve [EXHIBIT 9]

EXHIBIT 9   THE CHANGE CURVE

Morale and confidence are likely to rise and fall through the five stages of the change curve.

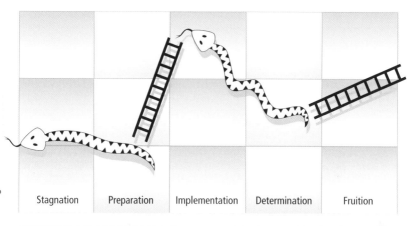

Organisationis morale and confidence

| Stagnation | Preparation | Implementation | Determination | Fruition |

Time

Source: Audit Commission adaptation of Jeanie Daniel Duck

I   *The Change Monster: The human forces that fuel or foil corporate transformation and change,* Jeanie Daniel Duck, 2001.

Stage 1: Stagnation

35. Overall performance is static or declining either in absolute terms, or relative to the market or to stakeholder expectations. Often a large number of low-level, unrelated performance improvement initiatives remain 'live', neither linked to each other nor to any central strategic vision, many having stalled or withered away without formal end points or tangible results. A large police authority, for example, recently commissioned external consultants to map all planned and current reviews of its police force. The consultants found several hundred, but no definitive list, nor any systematic way of managing or co-ordinating them. There was also a lack of clarity about what the reviews were trying to achieve and how recommendations would be implemented. At this stage it is quite common to find more improvement on paper than in reality – typically a proliferation of written strategies and plans with unrealistic milestones and little in the way of follow-up or accountability.

Stage 2: Preparation

36. At this stage, recognition typically dawns that overall performance is inadequate and continuing on the current trajectory is unacceptable. This may be the result of some kind of external scrutiny, possibly accompanied by the threat of punitive sanctions, including direct intervention and loss of control. It may come from listening to customers, providing an unexpected and unpleasant picture of your services from their perspective. This realisation, however it dawns, is normally accompanied by a sharp dip in morale. The next step is acceptance that change is needed, on a scale that implies significant upheaval rather than marginal improvement. It may be clear that this will be impossible to achieve with the current team, precipitating necessary but potentially destabilising changes at the top of the organisation. Once this phase is over, the senior team can focus on the central vision, setting targets for future performance and a plan for change, and establishing the central mechanisms and accountabilities to move things forward. This may mean dedicated project teams with some form of light touch co-ordination. As the teams kick off, creative potential is unleashed to generate bold ideas, which are approved by the leadership team for implementation. This creates a high level of energy and increasing sense that **this** change programme is going to make a difference, where many others have failed. At this point, morale can reach an artificially high point and unrealistic expectations can start to build.

Stage 3: Implementation

37. The rubber hits the road. Translating ideas into action is (always) tougher than expected. This is the point at which jobs may be lost. Some early wins may restore optimism about the programme as a whole. In other areas, teething difficulties suggest that original plans may need to be modified. The hard work of rebuilding supporting infrastructure and systems – information technology, human resources, people development, performance management – begins, and, at this stage, demands maximum effort for minimal immediate gain. The honeymoon period, if there was one, is over.

Stage 4: Determination

38. Mixed results from the first few months of implementation create an opening for serious doubts to creep in. The programme runs into significant organisational resistance and support begins to melt away. Other more 'urgent' priorities threaten to distract management attention and divert resources away from the change programme. External commentators and/or the local press may pick up and amplify individual instances where things have gone wrong, contributing to an undermining of confidence. Internally and externally, advocates of the programme and those most closely associated with it begin to feel nervous. Detractors sense an opening and prepare themselves for the counter-offensive. This is a critical point. Only determination and renewed, visible commitment from the top team will see the programme through this test.

Stage 5: Fruition

39. Gradually, even against the odds, the programme appears to be delivering. Operational changes are translated into real results that are noticed by customers, commentators and stakeholders. Perceptions of the organisation are changing, both externally and internally. The increased flexibility and power of new infrastructure begin to pay dividends on a broader front. Managers have internalised the overall vision and make use of delegated powers to experiment with new ideas. Limitations in the original blueprint for change are met by renewed creativity and better solutions. The capability and confidence built through the first wave of changes are embedded in the organisation, as key figures in the change programme return full time to their operational jobs or to new ones. Step-change has turned into continuous improvement.

KEY POINTS

Real change requires sustaining focus on the key priorities

- More change is achieved through doing fewer things well

- Organisations with a clear direction and some demonstrable results are better able to resist being deflected and distracted

- Persistence, resilience and consistency are critical to stay on track through the typical ups and downs of change

5. Focus on users

Understanding users

Involving users

Measuring what matters to users

Key points

Understanding users

40. A change programme to improve public services that does not begin and end with customers is unlikely to deliver its full potential, if indeed it delivers anything much at all. User focus does not, of course, imply that all customer demands can be satisfied. It is the role of the political process, whether local or national, to reconcile expectations of public services with the resources available to deliver them. This is, at best, an imperfect system, leaving the local leadership team deeply embroiled in managing the tension between potentially infinite and contradictory demands and finite resources. There will always be choices to be made. But the fact that the expressed needs of users are not themselves rational and mutually consistent is not a reason for avoiding objective investigation and analysis. Without knowing anything about the people who use your service, how can you begin to understand their needs? Without hearing what they want from you, how can you focus on the areas that really matter to them? Without an accurate picture of their experience, how can you be sure that you fully understand what works and what needs fixing, especially where your contribution is part of an extended process involving other agencies as well as your own [CASE STUDY 11]?

CASE STUDY 11   JOINING UP SERVICES FOR USERS

Background: The London Borough of Hammersmith and Fulham's housing department is developing and joining up its services to meet evolving client needs. In 1997, there was evidence of rising demand for support for tenants with mental health problems and dissatisfaction with existing service provision. Consultation showed that tenants were unhappy with mainstream services and wanted access to specialist support. At the same time, housing officers were worried by high rates of tenancy breakdown, with persistent problems of rent arrears and neighbour complaints. There was also concern from health and social services over the housing being offered to mental health clients leaving hospital.

Approach: A new Mental Health and HIV Housing Team was set up in 1998, bringing together staff from different functions to respond more flexibly to a wider range of client needs. A survey of mental health accommodation projects helped to establish a profile of clients and their needs. A hospital liaison officer was appointed to work closely with Charing Cross Hospital to meet the housing needs of in-patients and to prevent delays to hospital discharge. Performance indicators are now routinely used to track improvements and fine tune the service.

Impact: Over a three-year period, the number of new clients helped has more than doubled. The weekly total of benefits being paid following team intervention rose from £952 to £3,987 between 1998/99 and 1999/00, and rent arrears have reduced. Over the same period, hospital referrals provided with accommodation rose from 26 per cent to 46 per cent and the proportion helped to return to their own homes increased from 13 per cent to 27 per cent. Client surveys show high levels of satisfaction, and feedback from housing officers shows that they are much happier with the support they get in providing a service to tenants with mental health problems.

A more detailed review of supported mental health accommodation is now underway, as a result of a joint funding bid by the housing services department, social services department and Ealing, Hammersmith and Hounslow Health Authority.

Critical factors

* Keeping in touch with the changing needs of users
* Building partnerships with other agencies

41. Organisations develop their own internal belief systems that become invisibly embedded in everyday decisions and behaviour. These commonly include assumptions about who the customers are, what they think about the organisation, how and why they use services, and what they want and value [CASE STUDY 12, overleaf].

Background: In 1997, the Oxford Radcliffe Hospitals NHS Trust was among the poorest performing trusts in the Anglia and Oxford region, both for waiting times for surgery and the number of people on surgical waiting lists. Only 40 per cent of cataract surgery was performed as day cases, compared to the median for England of between 60 per cent and 70 per cent.

Approach: A team of ophthalmology staff (as described in case study 6) was given responsibility to reduce waiting times and lists. Their role was to analyse workload and demand, and identify solutions to make the service more efficient. Increasing the proportion of people treated as day surgery cases had the potential to alleviate pressure on in-patient wards and improve throughput.

The team issued questionnaires to ophthalmology service users. Results showed that patients were not choosing day case treatment because they had to return to hospital the following day. The questionnaire also revealed that patients living alone were particularly reluctant to undergo day surgery.

In response to user feedback, the ophthalmology department changed its practice so that people undergoing routine cataract surgery were no longer required to return to hospital the day after surgery. Telephone assessment clinics have been introduced before admission, and rather than excluding people living alone from the day surgery option, better information is given to all suitable patients about the day procedure, and how they can expect to feel and manage immediately afterward.

Monitoring user opinions has continued, overturning concerns from staff about elderly patients travelling home after dark after the newly introduced twilight operating sessions. Patients and their families reported that evening sessions were more convenient as family members were often able to escort patients to and from hospital when sessions fell outside normal working hours. In addition, patients treated outside peak periods valued the less frenetic environment.

Impact: Uptake of day case treatment has increased: 80 per cent of people having cataract treatment now return home the same day, instead of staying overnight in hospital.

Critical factors

- Staff cannot always predict users' preferences or responses to changes: direct user feedback tells staff what matters to them and why

- User involvement in change programmes can help to identify opportunities to improve service efficiency

- Ongoing feedback helps to ensure that efficiency initiatives are compatible with improving the quality of patient care

42. Without actively listening to customers and feeding that information back regularly and quickly to inform staff and management thinking, services can become dangerously out of touch. Listening to front-line staff within your own organisation, such as drivers, receptionists and others who have daily contact with customers, is often a good place to start.

43. Many private sector companies are building up increasingly sophisticated pictures of their customer base:

- distinguishing different types of customer with different profiles and needs (market segmentation);

- collecting live feedback;

- undertaking indepth research about customer behaviour and preferences; and

- using technology to track and analyse shopping habits.

Public services have other options available, including community consultation (a variety of approaches is described in an Audit Commission management paper,[1] which includes a pull-out wallchart setting out the pros and cons of different methods such as surveys, focus groups and panels). Many of the alternatives on offer are now well established and expertise is widely available. However, few public bodies fully exploit the potential that exists to develop a rich understanding of customer preferences and apply it in their service improvement initiatives [CASE STUDY 13, overleaf]

---

[1]   *Listen Up: Effective Community Consultation*, Audit Commission, 1999.

Background: Following the 1993 Department of Health paper, *Changing Childbirth*, the Audit Commission undertook national research[1] and audited the maternity services provided by individual NHS trusts throughout England and Wales. Each audit included a survey of the views of a random sample of new mothers to provide a user view of the services offered by the trust. The audit of Trafford Healthcare NHS Trust identified a number of areas needing improvement, including:

- unnecessarily long waits at antenatal appointments because some consultants were doing routine check-ups for 'low-risk' women;

- a lack of continuity of care, with support during delivery coming from a number of different people, rather than the same staff throughout, because rostering did not allow for continuous care; and

- poor continuity and consistency of care on postnatal wards because staff were being called away to assist busy labour wards.

Approach: A new clinical director and service manager of midwifery used external evidence from national guidance, reports and the user survey as levers to change clinical practice and move to a more mother-centred service. Key changes included:

- involving midwives in restructuring their service. Midwife teams now see women from designated local patches, so mothers can be supported by 'their' team both in the community and in hospital. Ward staff levels were increased and shift patterns changed so that the same staff can attend a woman through delivery and postnatally;

- developing a new protocol for 'low-risk' mothers, minimising antenatal appointments with consultants and seeing women in the community; and

- introducing regular medical audit. Peers are now able to highlight and challenge variations in their colleagues' practice.

I   *First Class Delivery: Improving Delivery Services in England and Wales,*
Audit Commission, 1997.

Impact: Activity data from the hospital and staff feedback show improvements across maternity services. Waits at antenatal clinics have reduced as many women attend clinic only twice. Many clinics are now held at local general practices. Women experience better continuity of care during and following delivery from less pressured staff.

Critical factors

* Asking mothers what they think of the service

* Challenging established practice with a range of external and internal information

Involving users

44. Leicester Royal Infirmary actively involved a panel of patients in the early stages of its re-engineering project. Volunteers tracked the pathway that patients followed through the hospital to complete routine diagnostic tests. This revealed that the total distance travelled by a typical patient between departments could be measured in miles. The patient panel described their ideal of a one-stop diagnostic appointment, where all necessary tests could be carried out in one session, by a single person. Their idea was turned into reality in the Balmoral Testing Centre, which is more efficient as well as more patient-friendly.

Measuring what matters to users

45. Thoroughly understanding customer experience provides the basis for setting targets and measuring the things that customers think are important, as well as the technical efficiency and effectiveness indicators that are the basis of a sound service. Moving through a change programme, it is important to keep checking that your vision and what you are delivering make sense to users and chime with what they consider to be important. That may be, for example, improved educational attainment and participation in the labour market or, alternatively, clean pavements, playground swings and street lights that work. In the case of accident and emergency services, the public may be just as concerned about how far it is to the nearest A&E department, how long they have to wait when they get there and whether the environment is clean and safe, as they are with survival and disability rates.

KEY POINTS

To deliver their full potential, change programmes need to begin and end with customers

- Service providers must understand what matters to their customers (users, patients, carers and the community), and how they experience the service

- Listening and objective evidence are essential to this understanding

- Performance targets should include the things that matter most to customers

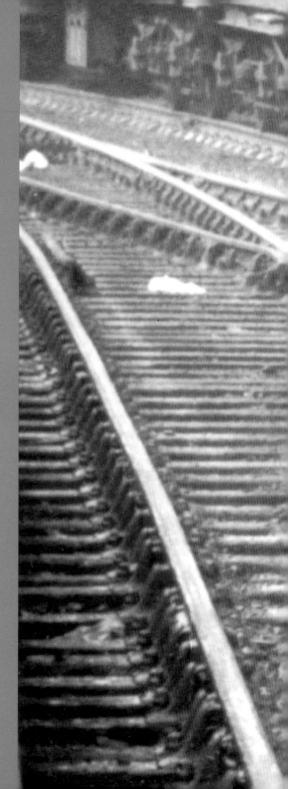

6. Managing the change programme

Project management

The balanced scorecard

Key points

Project management

46. Project management is important in any major change programme. Conceptually, this is probably the most straightforward phase: the local vision has been developed, the analysis completed, the big decisions made. All that remains is to put the agreed strategy into action. But significant change is inevitably complex, with multiple, cross-functional interdependencies and a confounding element of unpredictability. As with understanding user needs, adopting a systematic approach to implementation cannot in itself make messy, unpredictable reality magically simple and manageable. Major change is not a straightforward linear process, but managing the complexity is virtually impossible without a robust plan that is supported by strong project management [CASE STUDY 14].

CASE STUDY 14   RECOGNISING PROJECT MANAGEMENT AS KEY TO IMPLEMENTATION

Background: The Kings Mill Centre for Healthcare Services[1] had a serious and ongoing problem providing sufficient ward nurses. To ensure safe levels of staffing and avoid closing beds, the Trust became increasingly dependent on commercial agencies for temporary nursing staff. Even then, agencies could not provide enough staff to fill shifts, with the result that beds still had to be closed and operations cancelled.

Furthermore, reliance on agency nursing staff potentially exposed patients to increased clinical risk, because the Trust could not guarantee that agency nurses' skills were appropriate, regularly evaluated and updated. Continuity of patient care was also undermined.

The leadership team agreed that it had a problem, but not how to solve it. The situation affected all of them, but they lacked the information needed to make a decision and no individual could find sufficient time to work out and implement a satisfactory solution on behalf of the entire team.

Approach: The need for clear project management was addressed by bringing in a secondee with direct responsibility for:

* analysing the situation;

I   Now part of the Sherwood Forest Hospitals NHS Trust.

- developing a solution;

- getting the solution approved; and

- implementing the change in a structured way, against a clear project plan.

She had the support of the chief executive, giving her access to the leadership team and influence with other staff. She worked with other directors individually to deal with their concerns. A nurse manager was released to work with her part-time, providing clinical input and helping to build commitment from clinical staff.

Impact: Kings Mill opted to set up and run its own nurse bank, with a dedicated co-ordinator and computer support. As a result, the use of agency nursing staff has been all but eliminated and the proportion of shifts covered has significantly improved.

All bank nurses have access to training and regular performance appraisals. Attending the Trust induction programme ensures that they are familiar with the hospital's layout and procedures. These changes should reduce some of the clinical risks associated with temporary nursing staff.

Critical factors

- Focused attention

- Thorough planning and project management

- Chief executive support

- Clinical involvement

47. Few public sector organisations are over-endowed with strong project managers. Project management skills are being developed, but slowly, and many effective operational managers struggle when it comes to seeing through the delivery of complex projects. The essential skills are:

- being able to define the project and its boundaries in a way that is deliverable;

- breaking it down into manageable modules of work with outputs and deadlines;

- identifying the key cross links and dependencies;

- building and supporting effective project teams;
- providing a structure for planning and monitoring progress;
- identifying and negotiating the resources needed;
- communicating with senior management and other related projects;
- identifying and managing risk; and
- balancing clarity with flexibility.

Given a general shortage of these types of skills, planning a change programme should include identifying where in your organisation the strongest project management skills lie, how to deploy them in the most critical places and how, over the longer term, to acquire and build more.

48. Successful delivery needs rigorous planning, a systematic approach and thorough execution, balanced with flexibility, whatever the scale of the change being implemented [CASE STUDY 15]. In a major change programme, it rarely makes sense for the senior management team to control detailed project management. It is the role of the leadership team to provide the freedom and resources for managers to deliver their part of the changes, together with accountability for challenging targets and deadlines, negotiated with and owned by those responsible for delivering them. This enables more leadership time to be invested in the critical selling and communications activities that are essential to the success of the programme.

CASE STUDY 15   PROFESSIONALISM AND RELENTLESS RIGOUR TURN AROUND A FAILING SCHOOL

Background: St George's Catholic School in Maida Vale hit the headlines in 1995 when its headmaster was murdered outside the gates trying to protect one of his pupils from a gang of truants. After three subsequent years of falling standards and deteriorating discipline, St George's was temporarily closed for the safety of both pupils and staff. OFSTED put the school in special measures and a new headmistress was brought out of retirement and given a year to turn the school around.

Approach: Staff helped to select a mission statement that reflected the school's underlying spiritual values. The mission was constantly reinforced and applied as the lens through which any changes were tested, by asking "How will this improve the children's education or development?" The new leadership brought many innovations, instilling a profound belief in the value of every individual as well as making school a much more positive and fulfilling experience. The energy and ideas were underpinned by a highly professional and rigorous management approach, designed to deliver tangible improvements within a very tight timescale. The mission statement was the basis for establishing mutual expectations and clear lines of accountability. Both staff and children were given clear responsibilities; they were encouraged to deliver and their performance was actively monitored and fed back to them. All teachers were expected to adopt a planned and structured approach to lessons, with learning objectives and tasks written up at the start of every lesson and reviewed at the end. Clear procedures were established for preparing and reviewing lesson plans. Those who could or would not accept the new systems moved on. Heads of year were expected to chase attendance and every student group had targets with graphs of how they were actually doing displayed for all the children to see, harnessing their competitive spirit to drive the figures up.

Impact: Three months after the new leadership had taken over, OFSTED reported significant progress, with most behaviour satisfactory, attendance rising, working methods developing well and the school a more stimulating and vibrant environment in which to learn. One year on from the introduction of special measures, they were withdrawn on the basis of greatly improved standards of teaching and learning, attendance approaching national averages and an atmosphere of respect for authority and pride in the school with pupils as positive, active learners.

Critical factors

- Strict, positive regime, with clear expectations, grounded on a strong set of values
- Relentless rigour in implementation

The balanced scorecard

49. To establish a framework for change and let the rest of the organisation get on with making things happen, the top team needs a shared high-level picture of the change journey and a view of the end results. You also need the monitoring mechanisms – like the gauges on complex equipment – that allow you to check that things are moving in the right direction at roughly the speed you expect, and that there are no major surprising adverse reactions appearing in the system. This monitoring function can be performed by the balanced scorecard [EXHIBIT 10]

EXHIBIT 10   THE BALANCED SCORECARD

The balanced scorecard can help organisations to manage performance.

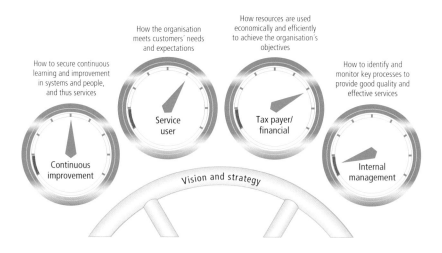

Source: Audit Commission adaptation of Kaplan & Norton

50. The balanced scorecard was developed by Kaplan and Norton[I] to help organisations to translate their vision and strategy into a coherent set of objectives, actions and performance measures, which they can use to manage their performance. The approach looks at performance from four inter-related dimensions: the customer or service user perspective; internal business processes; continuous improvement; and financial performance, and can be adapted to meet an organisation's specific needs.[II] A high-level scorecard should contain a mix of measures that, together, provide a rounded picture of progress and performance against the organisation's strategic goals. These measures need to be the best barometers of performance in the most critical areas, and offer advanced warning of where things may be going wrong. That means process (causal) as well as outcome indicators, and measures of internal staff attitudes and morale as well as customer satisfaction. Further down the organisation, managers need more detailed scorecards covering their own areas of responsibility. The contents of these more detailed scorecards should be linked clearly to the high-level scorecard.

51. In local government, scorecards can be constructed from a combination of best value performance indicators (BVPIs) and locally defined performance measures [CASE STUDY 16, overleaf]. The NHS Plan[III] is intended to result in more meaningful and better quality performance information for the health service, with local bodies constructing annual report cards to inform the public of their performance. As more relevant and better quality data become available, organisations will need to distinguish the information that management needs to run the business from that aimed at the public about the things that are important to them. Equally, as the visions and strategies of local bodies change over time, incorporating, for example, an increased emphasis on improving the life experiences of

Managing the change programme

79

The balanced scorecard

I   *The Balanced Scorecard: Measures that Drive Performance*, Kaplan and Norton, 1992.

II More information on the balanced scorecard can be found in *The Measures of Success: Developing a Balanced Scorecard to Measure Performance*, Accounts Commission, 1998.

III *NHS Plan: A Plan for Investment, A Plan for Reform*, Department of Health, 2000.

local people, scorecards will need to evolve to reflect this. Guidance on designing and reviewing performance information systems can be found in a recent joint report by the National Audit Office, Audit Commission, Cabinet Office, Office for National Statistics and HM Treasury.[I]

CASE STUDY 16   USING A BALANCED SCORECARD TO ASSESS PERFORMANCE

Background: Newcastle City Council is using the balanced scorecard to help to provide a rounded picture of performance that is clearly linked to its strategic objectives.

Approach: The council consulted internally about how the scorecard's four dimensions should be presented, and decided that categories for democratic accountability, good stewardship, continuous improvement and organisational development best suited its needs.

The concept was explained to staff at a series of seminars during 2000, and a senior staff workshop developed a set of indicators that linked the council's objectives to the four dimensions of the scorecard, combining best value performance indicators (BVPIs) and local performance measures.

The corporate team added to the indicators, producing a detailed set of measures for assessing the performance of individual directorates. The high-level scorecard was built from a subset of measures that related most closely to the corporate vision, and uses eight indicators for organisational development and five for each of the other quadrants.

A traffic light system highlights performance against scorecard targets – green where a target has been achieved, yellow for good progress short of the target and red where no progress is evident. The council plans to monitor targets regularly and report performance quarterly to the corporate team. The first assessment identified clear progress in three of the areas, but showed that staff development activities had not yet delivered improvements, highlighting this as an area needing attention.

I   *Choosing the Right Fabric: A Framework for Performance Information*, National Audit Office, Audit Commission, Cabinet Office, Office for National Statistics and HM Treasury, 2001.

Democratic accountability

How much do stakeholders think that
their views are taken into account?

Measures include:

Percentage of citizens satisfied
with overall service provided by
their authority (BVPI)

Percentage of population
who feel that their views can
influence service provision (Local)

Continuous improvement

How are services improving
on the ground?

Measures include:

General satisfaction of
residents measured against
basket of BVPIs

Implementation of BV review
programme and percentage of targets
reached in BV action plans (Local)

Good stewardship

Are the council's services efficient?

Measures include:

Percentage of council tax
collected (BVPI)

Clear strategic links between
corporate policy, asset management
and investment in services (Local)

Organisational development

Are staff being trained and supported
to do a good job?

Measures include:

The level of the CRE's
'Standard for Local Government' to
which the authority conforms (BVPI)

Percentage of staff who feel
that their work is valued (Local)

Note: BVPI relates to best value performance indicators as specified by the DTLR.

Newcastle plans to adopt the balanced scorecard as its main organisational performance measurement tool. Performance appraisals for the chief executive and directors have been aligned with the scorecard, and some directorates have made progress towards their own scorecards. There are plans to look more closely at how measures at all levels of the organisation can link together effectively, and to refine the framework with experience.

Impact: The council believes that developing the scorecard has:

- helped staff to see the big picture and devote attention to customer satisfaction and staff development as well as to costs and service quality;

- broadened the set of indicators used, to include 'soft' local measures that are key to longer-term service performance; and

- triggered productive discussions across the organisation about measurement and improvement.

Critical factors

- Tailoring the scorecard to meet the organisation's own specific needs
- Building buy-in by involving staff
- Comprehensive follow-through to include monitoring systems and individual performance appraisal

KEY POINTS

Strong project management is needed to deliver durable change

- Significant change is complex, with many cross-functional dependencies
- Delivery requires rigorous planning and thorough execution, balanced with flexibility
- The leadership team is responsible for setting the framework
  - providing authority and resources
  - setting challenging targets and deadlines
  - tracking the change journey
  - keeping focused on end results whilst listening to progress on the ground

7. Using external help

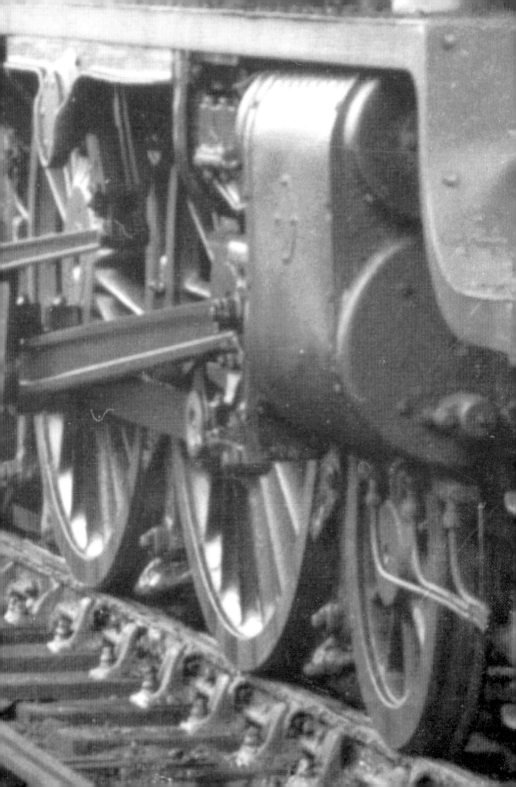

Making the best use of 'outsiders'

52. People from outside your organisation can help you on your change journey. There are many organisations to choose from, and with the current appetite for new and different types of 'regulation', increasing numbers do not find it neccessary to wait for an invitation. External input, whether voluntary or imposed, can play a useful role, although there are clearly downsides, too. Any form of external involvement, however valuable, places its own demands on the organisation and needs to be managed in a conscious and constructive way to extract the maximum benefit. Your organisation is most likely to benefit if you already have an accurate picture of your own performance and a clear sense of direction. This provides the basis for developing a shared understanding of what needs to be done, so that you can help to shape the external agency's involvement from a position of knowledge.

53. External input to change programmes can take several different forms, including professional advice, peer or consultancy support, regulatory scrutiny, and involvement from the community and voluntary sectors. Each of these has a distinct role to play, but some of the common benefits of external input include:

- an objective view of your performance, based on some combination of new data or analysis, comparison with others and knowledge of what works elsewhere;

- the ability to gather and feed back others' views of your organisation and the service it provides, including customers, staff and other stakeholders, who may be more reluctant to report directly to you in an open and honest way;

- professional experience and judgement coupled with a fresh perspective; and

- a constructive challenge to implicit internal beliefs and assumptions.

Professional, peer and consultancy support may also provide:

- specific skills that are in short supply, which you may find difficult to source directly or may need only for a specific short-term task or time period, such as information technology;

- technical advice and expertise in areas such as developing role definitions and appraisal systems;

- coaching and counselling to key people to help them to overcome barriers to change and develop vital skills such as feedback and managing underperformance;

- impartial and expert facilitation of your own staff; and

- experience of supporting successful change.

The remainder of this section will focus on the role of regulation and other professional advice and support for change programmes.

The role of regulation

54. The activities of regulators, including auditors and inspectors, offer potential for constructive challenge. Both the prospect and the reality of scrutiny can be a spur to change. At their best, inspectors and others can provide your organisation and the public you serve with an independent view of your services and the likelihood that you will succeed in improving them. External reviewers can identify opportunities for improvement and make recommendations to help you to achieve better performance. Whether this is translated into positive results is down to the way in which you respond [CASE STUDY 17]. Evidence from many sectors demonstrates that imposed change tends to create powerful resistance, so there are substantial barriers to building durable change on the back of external intervention. The key learning from organisations that have succeeded in delivering sustained improvement with regulators as catalysts is the need for the leadership team to own the messages and build support for change, communicating and engaging with staff and stakeholders throughout the process.

EXTERNAL SCRUTINY AS A SPUR TO CHANGE   CASE STUDY 17

Background: In 1999, Torfaen Social Services received a highly critical review from a joint inspection by the Audit Commission and Social Services Inspectorate for Wales (SSIW). The review team was particularly concerned that:

- some standards of professional practice were unacceptably poor, particularly sometimes in children's services;

- social services were not well organised to plan and deliver much needed service improvement and change, resulting in a sense of drift;

- there appeared to be a lack of leadership and direction from politicians and management; and

- the relationship between front-line staff and managers was characterised by mutual mistrust and lack of confidence.

Approach: The review highlighted deep-seated problems in Torfaen and provided clear evidence that change was needed. Information came from a survey of over 100 users and carers, interviews with front-line staff, managers, partner organisations and politicians, observing management and practice on the ground, and analysing 60 case files.

Local momentum for change began to build even during the review. A critical turning point came when corporate and political leaders took ownership of the issues in social services. New departmental leadership started the programme of improvement. Since then, the Audit Commission and SSIW have monitored progress closely with local staff, to:

- establish accountability for change at manager and team level;

- suggest clear priorities for improvement;

- guide the direction of change;

- provide targets; and

- keep up the momentum and praise success.

Using information and action points from the review as a starting point, managers have focused on teams to get the 'basics' in place. They have developed staff accountability for carefully prioritised, deliverable 'chunks' of change, matched to their own interests and personal development needs. Managers are better informed about what is going on at all levels. Torfaen is developing better family support for children at risk and community-based options for social care.

Impact: The whole council now accepts the agenda for improvement and is better organised to plan and deliver it. Senior staff at Torfaen describe the changes following the review as "painful but positive". A recent follow-up review by the SSIW shows that social services continue to move in the right direction and special follow-up monitoring is no longer considered necessary.

Critical factors

• External scrutiny, demonstrating strong evidence of poor services

• Management ownership of change programme

• Delegation with accountability

55. Auditors and inspectors are required to make judgements and report on particular aspects of performance such as financial probity, management and governance arrangements, service quality and likelihood of improvement. Beyond these very specific responsibilities, they are also in a position to provide valuable support and advice to local bodies that are going through change, from their knowledge of the organisation, their professional skills and experience, and their exposure to good practice elsewhere. This role, however, must be compatible with the overriding requirement for regulators to retain their independence and objectivity in making judgements about the performance of the body.

Professional advice and support for change

56. Any major change programme is likely to need expert help of one kind or another. External advisers, including regulators, can play a supportive role. The Audit Commission has published a guide to the use of management consultants.[I] Many local bodies use their auditors to review areas of potential for improvement, outside the core risk-based audit, where they have relevant skills and expertise to offer. This frequently includes diagnostic tools, objective analysis and comparative performance data drawn from similar bodies [CASE STUDY 18, overleaf].

I   *Reaching the Peak: Getting Value for Money from Management Consultants,*
     Audit Commission/HMSO, 1994 – only available on the Audit Commission website.

Background: St Helens and Knowsley Trust Hospital used the results of a review by the auditor of hospital catering as part of its ongoing drive to develop services and improve patient satisfaction.

A patient survey highlighted dissatisfaction with the Trust's meal service; menus were considered to be repetitive and unpalatable. Menus were repeated weekly on an assumption that the average length of stay at the Trust was three days, but data showed that approximately 25 per cent of patient stays at one unit exceeded one week and, at another unit, the majority of patients were long-term.

Approach: Following the review, a multidisciplinary catering group was formed with patient representatives, nursing and catering staff. Popular dishes, identified by the survey, were introduced to replace some of the least popular meals. The group also changed the menu from a one-week to a two-week cycle and introduced a quarterly patient satisfaction survey to maintain the success of the programme.

Impact: Results show that patients are very happy with the new service and much prefer it to the old system.

Critical factors

- Understanding user preferences
- Help from external advisers

57. One of the most valuable things that external support can bring is the potential for skills transfer, so that when experts move on, capacity within your own organisation has increased. Both the Improvement and Development Agency (IDeA) in local government and the Modernisation Agency in the NHS explicitly define skills transfer as an objective in their work with local organisations.

Using external help

Professional advice and support for change

KEY POINTS

External input can contribute to making change happen

- 'Outsiders' offer a range of skills and can play a wide variety of roles

- Outside involvement adds most value when it results in organisations building their own internal capacity

- Organisations with a clear sense of direction are better placed to benefit from external input, even where it is uninvited or unwelcome

8. Building capacity for continuous improvement

Aiming for change-friendliness

58. If public services are to remain relevant, the pressure for change will never diminish. In a world of continuous, rapid, unpredictable change, public service organisations need to become change-friendly to survive. This implies doing more than simply sustaining gains that are made, though even this is challenging. It means getting better at change through actually doing it. If change-friendliness is recognised as an explicit goal from the start, it can be incorporated into the change programme [CASE STUDY 19]

CASE STUDY 19   BUILDING AN INFORMATION PLATFORM FOR CHANGE

Background: The police estate has not always kept pace with changing policing styles and public expectations of a modern, accessible service. Outdated buildings in the wrong place, unsuited to supporting new policing methods, can seriously hamper police effectiveness. The Government's 1997 comprehensive spending review identified asset management as a potential area for improved efficiency. Lack of management information about the extent and nature of land and property holdings owned by police authorities was a serious obstacle to a more strategic approach. The police service therefore agreed to work with the Audit Commission to develop the information base needed for major ongoing change.

Approach: A national study[1] involving property managers from all 43 forces in England and Wales developed a database of all property held by authorities. It also developed a suite of around 30 cost, space and quality benchmarks that forces could use to measure and compare performance.

The police property managers group agreed to take over the database after the Audit Commission's report was published. A benchmarking consultant, specialising in estate management, was recruited to maintain the database, handle updates and produce an annual report for members of the club.

1   *Action Stations: Improving Management of the Police Estate*, Audit Commission, 1999.

He also advises them on how best to adjust data so forces can compare performance with those with similar estate profiles. Individual forces can ask for reports that identify high-cost or inefficient buildings or track trends within and between command areas.

Impact: Forces are now using this information in a range of ways to deliver improved performance. Northamptonshire Police, for example, has targeted £5 million worth of property as surplus and has an action plan for tackling sites with high rateable values and/or high electricity costs. The force's estates strategy includes energy reduction targets that are calculated using benchmark reports. It also has outside help to develop a model to identify underused space in buildings.

All forces now have access to comprehensive information about their estates. This is helping them to take a more active approach to managing assets, releasing land for disposal and allowing reinvestment in priority facilities that are better suited to the needs of modern policing.

Critical factors

- Ongoing facility for assessing performance built into the change programme, to provide potential for future improvement

- Ownership from key stakeholders

Modernising infrastructure

59. Any programme that leads to step-change in performance will almost certainly come up against the limitations of the organisation, placing new and different demands on decision-making processes, information technology platforms, human resource functions, industrial relations, technical, management and leadership skills, the way you deal with customers and the information you use to run your business. All these implications add time, cost and complexity, but by recognising and responding to the challenges, you are equipping your organisation to navigate future waves of change. Infrastructure effects are likely to include the need for:

- increased delegation and faster decision-making processes;

- modernising outdated information and communications technology;

- more flexible human resource policies and procedures to attract, motivate, reward and retain the staff whom you need to deliver the business [CASE STUDY 20];

- increased emphasis on people and skills development;

- better internal communications systems to keep staff informed and maintain an ongoing constructive dialogue;

- more effective performance management systems;

- richer and more up-to-date management information, including customer and community intelligence;

- front-line customer interfaces that are better able to respond to queries and meet customers' needs effectively;

- building and sharing knowledge between different parts of your organisation and with partners;

- managing cross-cutting processes in a joined up way; and

- the ability to manage new kinds of relationships with unions and external partners.

CASE STUDY 20   REDESIGNING RECRUITMENT TO SERVE THE NEW BUSINESS

Background: Older people prefer to live in their own homes rather than in hospital or in long-stay residential care. Dudley Social Services is responding to this challenge by refocusing its services to support people living at home and reducing the need for residential care (as described in case study 5).

This has meant implementing a wide range of new initiatives, requiring many small changes to supporting processes as well as transforming direct care. One critical step was the recruitment of a new wave of home care staff, who better reflected the local community and could offer the practical skills and life experiences to meet the demands of the new role.

Approach: Given the nature of the local population, Dudley believed that the caring, 'can do' staff they needed ought to be available, but encouraging enough people to apply for the new posts presented a challenge. The skills involved in conventional recruitment procedures are very different from what is required for good home care staff. So the directorate took a fresh look at its

Modernising infrastructure   ` Building capacity for continuous improvement

recruitment process, launching high-profile local advertising campaigns for home care assistants, and using popular local venues and media. Staff at all levels of the directorate shared a big commitment to several open days. They took over whole training centres, with people from community services on hand to talk to and answer questions, help applicants fill in forms on the spot and proceed to interviews the same day. Applicants "did not have time to worry about an interview" and found the event "very helpful".

Impact: The success of the new approach is measurable, with a one-day event delivering 50 completed interviews and 24 successful appointments. Dudley now has a recruitment process that enables it to attract and employ people with the right skills to meet the future needs of its developing home care service.

Critical factors

• Redesigning a key support process to enable ongoing service improvement

• Willingness to experiment

60. One capability that is currently very much in the spotlight is the ability to build new kinds of relationship – both internally and externally, between different parts of your own organisation, with voluntary sector, commercial and public service partners, and with bodies that represent your staff. Modern approaches to performance management, which allow for greater freedom alongside clear accountability for performance, imply new types of relationship between the centre and operational units. Organisations also need to understand their own processes from the point of view of the customer in order to manage them in a joined up way, as they cross traditional boundaries. Building effective partnerships with other bodies is also a key capability that can emerge from a change programme [CASE STUDY 21, overleaf]. As partnerships become an increasingly important feature of the public services scene, you may find an Audit Commission management paper[I] helpful.

I   *A Fruitful Partnership: Effective Partnership Working*, Audit Commission, 1998.

Background: Derbyshire Police used best value processes to review its services to people experiencing domestic violence and child abuse. The team drew on a wide range of internal and external information, including activity and outcome data; surveys of officers, other agencies and people who had experienced domestic violence; and benchmarking against other forces.

Before the review, each division had separate domestic violence and child protection units, generally with different line managers and locations. The existing structures and working practices caused problems such as:

- mismatches between staffing levels and demand in different parts of the force area, leading to variable service;

- specialist domestic violence officers undertaking tasks that could be handled more efficiently by civilian support staff;

- a lack of intelligence-sharing between domestic violence and child protection staff;

- inadequate line management support within divisions due to pressure on senior time; and

- underinvestment in building partnerships with other agencies.

Approach: The review team recommended that the domestic violence and child protection units be merged into four family units, based on divisions but with centralised line management from headquarters. Child protection staffing levels were reduced and administrative tasks civilianised so that domestic violence officers were freed up for proactive work and special projects. These changes provided:

- improved service for users, increasing force-wide capacity and flexibility at no extra cost;

- better management and support for staff with demanding specialist roles; and

- more effective networking with other agencies.

Senior level support from the best value board (which included the chief constable and deputy leader of the police authority) meant that changes could

Building capacity for continuous improvement

Modernising infrastructure

be implemented very quickly – approval for the restructuring was given in August 1999, and the family units were set up in October and staff redeployed by the beginning of January 2000.

Impact: Activity data for the first year show that fewer child protection officers have handled a larger number of cases without increased overtime. Officer morale has improved: "We had low status before…now it's easier to get things done" (constable working in family unit), and information on families is more readily shared. Improved support has given the force capacity to introduce initiatives such as the Killingbeck domestic violence model, which grades responses to incidents, targeting resources where they are most needed and likely to be effective. It is early days for the project, but already "we've had lots of praise from victims" (DCI manager of family unit). New partnerships have been established with the health sector, including a domestic violence referral scheme with a major A&E department. "Domestic violence victims do often open up to us and tell us the truth, but before we lacked the skills and knowledge to deal with it. Now we have procedures in place…I can't stress how much it's helped us" (manager, A&E department).

Critical factors

- Thorough, objective review of current performance
- Visible and committed senior level support
- Targeting resources in line with user needs
- Creating a basis for partnerships with other agencies

Developing people

61. Effective public services require good leadership at many levels, not just at the very top. Although identifying and nurturing leadership talent is a key responsibility of senior teams, it can be a casualty of the pressures of operational survival. Change programmes can be a powerful way to extend skills and to develop future leaders by creating new leadership roles outside the formal organisational structure. Highlighting leadership development at the outset as a desirable outcome from the change increases the chances of achieving it. By their nature temporary, team and project leadership tasks can be assigned to targeted individuals without all the formality of conventional appointment procedures (although clearly this should not be a mandate for arbitrary selection or discrimination).

62. Giving able and committed people a chance to prove their capacity in demanding change roles can be highly motivating and benefit both the individual and the organisation. The key to making this work is:

- agreeing a set of stretching targets;

- providing the authority and resources to do the job;

- offering appropriate support; and

- recognising effort and achievement and aligning reward systems with the goals and values that motivate staff.

Incentive systems

63. Giving people ownership of performance targets, supported by appropriate incentives and rewards, is key to managing performance and individual behaviour with the direction of the change programme. Clearly this can only work where staff accept the targets assigned to them and have the authority and resources to deliver. A study by the Public Management Foundation[1] shows that public sector managers have different motivations from their private sector counterparts, distinguishing between a public sector ethos driven by the prospect of benefits for service users and the community, and a private sector focus on internal organisational goals and personal reward. It cautions against importing systems of reward and incentives from other sectors, particularly models that place heavy reliance on financial incentives. Instead, it encourages organisations to find out more about what motivates their staff, and review their performance assessment systems to reflect these factors.

---

[1] *Wasted Values: Harnessing the Commitment of Public Managers*, Public Management Foundation, 1999.

KEY POINTS

Step-change can be used to build the capacity for continuous improvement

- Organisations get better at change by doing it

- Major change programmes impact on core systems such as information technology, human resources and performance management – modernising these in line with the overall vision provides a platform for ongoing future change

- Change programmes are a powerful way to develop the leaders of the future

9. Conclusion

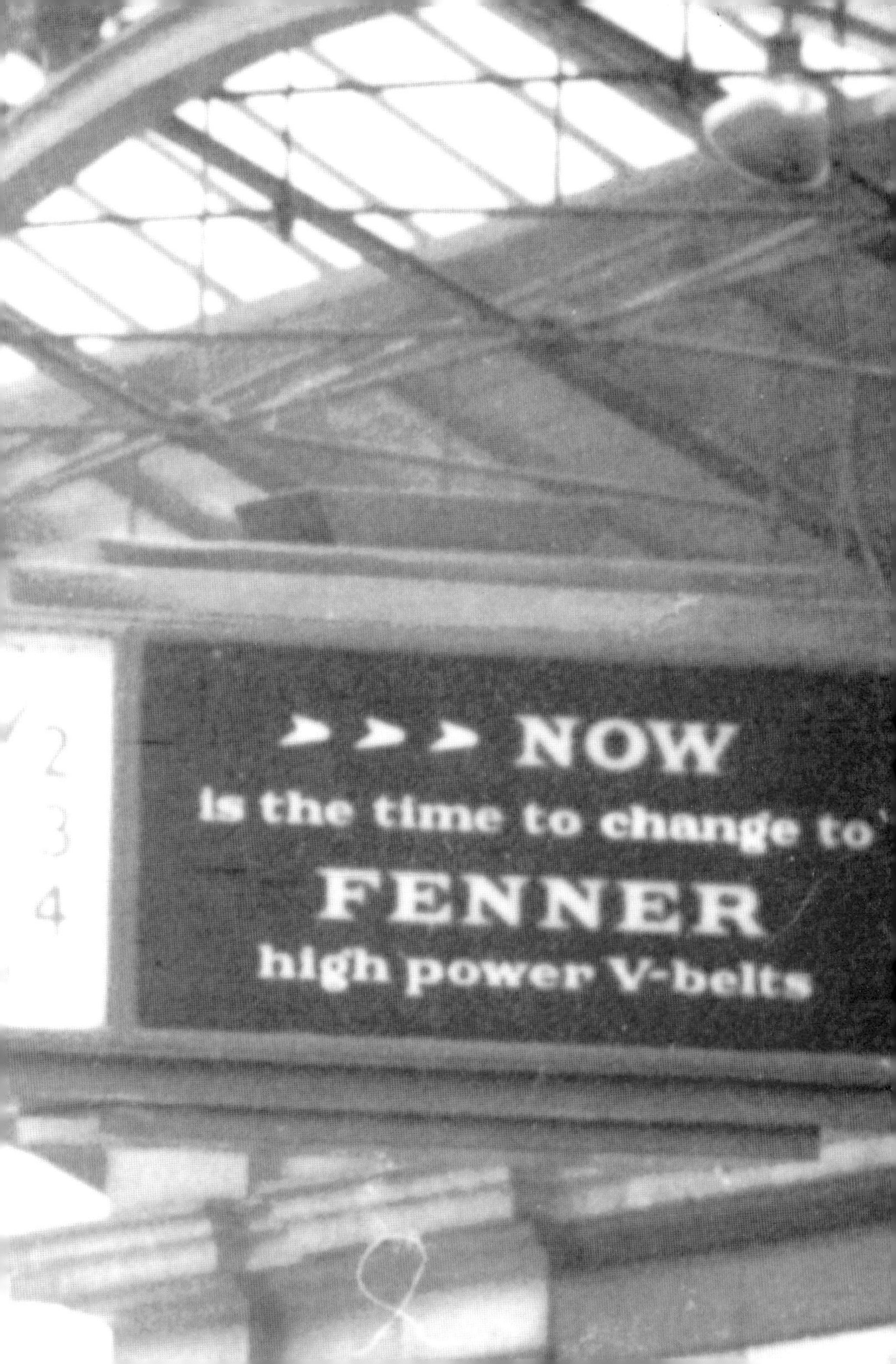
NOW
is the time to change to
FENNER
high power V-belts

64. Managing change is one of the greatest challenges faced by leadership teams in the modern world. Public service leaders are struggling with conflicting demands and unrealistic expectations from politicians, the public and their own staff. Meanwhile, the external environment is changing faster and less predictably than ever. In most parts of the public sector, incremental gains will be insufficient to satisfy political and public expectations. This combination of conditions – the need for step-gains in performance in an increasingly uncertain world – calls for the most demanding type of change. Leadership teams that set out to create the capability for continuous improvement through an initial step-change in performance are well placed to steer their organisations through the messy and difficult business of change. There is certainly no magic formula, but there is a body of useful experience about what works, drawn from both public and private sectors, that can be of value to top management in improving services today and building long-term capacity for the future.

65. The Audit Commission is very interested to learn more about the experiences of public service leaders who manage change. In deepening its understanding of change management issues, the Commission hopes to make a continuing contribution to practice in this field, and also to refine and develop its own approaches to supporting public service improvement. If you have any feedback on this paper, or would like to share your own organisation's experience of the change process, please contact the Commission's Performance Development Directorate by letter, telephone or email to changehere@audit-commission.gov.uk.

Appendix

Acknowledgements

The project was supported by an advisory group which provided invaluable assistance. The Commission is also grateful to local services and auditors and inspectors who helped us to develop case studies, and to those organisations and individuals who offered their advice and comments on drafts of the report. As always, the responsibility for the content of the report rests with the Commission alone.

Advisory group members

Helen Dawson   *Director of Learning and Development*
                       Improvement and Development Agency

Nigel Edwards   *Policy Director*
                       NHS Confederation

Professor Ewan Ferlie *Research Director*
                       Imperial College Management School

Dr Naomi Fulop   *Director*
                       National Co-ordinating Centre for
                       NHS Service Delivery and Organisation
                       Research & Development

Cynthia Griffin   *Director of Best Practice*
                       Improvement and Development Agency
                       (now Executive Director, Customer Access
                       and Services, London Borough of Havering)

Maggie Jones   *Policy Practice and Development Manager*
                       Joseph Rowntree Foundation

Matthew Warburton   *Head of Strategy*
                       Local Government Association

The team

The project was directed by Joanne Shaw. The project team comprised Cressy Bridgeman (project manager), Karen Naya and Julie O'Donnell. The report was designed by Gareth Sully.

References

NHS Plan: A Plan for Investment, A Plan for Reform, Department of Health, 2000.

Organisational Change: A review for managers, professionals and researchers, Valerie Iles and Kim Sutherland, National Co-ordinating Centre for NHS Service Delivery and Organisation, 2001.

Transforming the Organisation: New approaches to management, measurement and leadership, Keith Ruddle and David Feeny, Templeton College, 1997.

Strengthening Leadership in the Public Sector, Performance and Innovation Unit, Cabinet Office, 2001.

The Coming of Age: Improving Care Services for Elderly People, Audit Commission, 1997.

Trading Places: The Supply and Allocation of School Places, Audit Commission, 1996.

Listen Up: Effective Community Consultation, Audit Commission, 1999.

The Change Monster: The human forces that fuel or foil corporate transformation and change, Jeanie Daniel Duck, 2001.

First Class Delivery: Improving Delivery Services in England and Wales, Audit Commission, 1997.

The Balanced Scorecard – Measures that Drive Performance, Robert S. Kaplan and David P. Norton, Harvard Business Review, 1992.

The Measures of Success: Developing a Balanced Scorecard to Measure Performance, Accounts Commission, 1998.

Choosing the Right Fabric: A Framework for Performance Information, National Audit Office, Audit Commission, Cabinet Office, Office for National Statistics and HM Treasury, 2001.

Reaching the Peak: Getting Value for Money from Management Consultants, Audit Commission/HMSO, 1994 – only available on the Audit Commission website.

Action Stations: Improving Management of the Police Estate, Audit Commission, 1999.

A Fruitful Partnership: Effective Partnership Working, Audit Commission, 1998.

Wasted Values: Harnessing the Commitment of Public Managers, Jane Steele, Public Management Foundation, 1999.